SIL SPEAKS

Teilhard de Chardin, Yves Congar, John Courtney Murray, and Thomas Merton

ROBERT NUGENT

PAULIST PRESS
New York/Mahwah, NJ

Cover design by Joy Taylor
Book design by Lynn Else

Copyright © 2011 by Robert Nugent.

Library of Congress Cataloging-in-Publication Data

Nugent, Robert, SDS.
    Silence speaks : Teilhard de Chardin, Yves Congar, John Courtney Murray, and Thomas Merton / Robert Nugent.
        p. cm.
    Includes bibliographical references (p.   ).
    ISBN 978-0-8091-4649-9 (alk. paper)
    1. Teilhard de Chardin, Pierre. 2. Congar, Yves, 1904–1995. 3. Murray, John Courtney. 4. Merton, Thomas, 1915–1968. 5. Church controversies—Catholic Church—History—20th century. 6. Catholic Church—Teaching office—History—20th century. 7. Catholic Church—Doctrines—History—20th century. I. Title.
    BX1795.C69.N85 2011
    230′.20922—dc22

                                                                                2010021722

Published by Paulist Press
997 Macarthur Boulevard
Mahwah, New Jersey 07430

www.paulistpress.com

Printed and bound in the United States of America

Cromwell: You refused the oath tendered to you at the Tower...

More: Silence is not denial...

Cromwell: Because this silence betokened—nay, this silence **was** not silence at all but most eloquent denial.

More: Not so, Master Secretary, the maxim is "qui tacet consentire." The maxim of the law is "Silence gives consent." If, therefore, you wish to construe what my silence "betokened," you must construe that I consented, not that I denied.

Thomas More (1477–1535) in
A Man for all Seasons by Robert Bolt

The last chalice, should our dear Lord ever proffer this one to you, comes to you when obstacles are laid in your path by those very persons who are appointed by God to support and protect you, even by ecclesiastical authority itself. This is the fourth and the bitterest chalice.

Father Francis Mary of the Cross Jordan (1848–1918),
Founder of the Society of the Divine Savior

I love the Church because Christ loved it, love it to her utmost extreme. I love it even when I discover painful attitudes and structures, which I do not find in harmony with Gospel. I love it as it is because Christ also loved me with all my imperfections, with all my shadows and constantly gives me the first fruits of the Kingdom so that my love may correspond to his eternal plan....Christ and the Church with him remind me of all the limitless evidence of love, grace and mercy. In this the Church helps me to form a grateful memory. If we open ourselves to this and gratefully remember all the good, which has flowed to us in the Church, and constantly flows to us, then we can and will all succeed in giving even the suffering from the Church its place in the heart of Jesus.

Father Bernard Haring, CSsR (1912–1998),
My Witness for the Church

...a minimalist standard of non-contradiction has been replaced by a maximalist standard that requires not only theologians but pastors to present a range of specified points of Catholic teaching around a given issue, and to do so in precisely the language prescribed by Vatican authorities. Now people are being silenced **not** for contradicting any doctrine, and not even for contradicting "noninfallible teaching," but for staying within church teaching while not equally emphasizing or including other points.

Lisa Sowle Cahill, *America*, August 14, 1999

CONTENTS

To Dr. David Gentry-Akin, longtime friend,
Louvain colleague, theologian and professor at
St. Mary's College, Moraga, California,
whose untiring commitment to preserving and
nourishing a Catholic identity and tradition,
both personally and among his friends and students,
has provided me support and wisdom in discerning
the value and meaning of silence—both
imposed and freely chosen.

ACKNOWLEDGMENTS

The chapters in this book are revised and expanded versions of essays that, with the permission of my religious superiors, previously appeared in other journals. The author and publisher kindly acknowledge those journals for their gracious permission to use them in this work.

"From Silence to Vindication: Teilhard de Chardin and the Holy Office" first appeared in *Commonweal*, October 25, 2002; "Yves Congar: Apostle of Patience" first appeared in the *Australian E-Journal of Theology*, February 2005; "The Silenced Monk" first appeared in *America*, May 15, 2006; "The Censuring of John Courtney Murray" first appeared in two parts in *The Catholic World* for January–February 2008 and March–April 2008.

The author would also like to express his appreciation to John Allen, David Bergner, SDS, Francis DeBernardo, Richard Hite, Leon Hooper, SJ, Joseph Komonchak, Mary and John Linton, Paul Pearson, Steven Schloesser, SJ, and Andrew Urbanski, SDS, for their major and minor contributions.

Special and sincere thanks to Dr. Richard Gaillardetz for his insightful Introduction. I am honored to have him provide historical background and suggestions for the future that puts the lives and work of these four giants in context and points the way for a more transparent and just process

Silence Speaks

for the magisterium. I consider Dr. Gaillardetz, as one of the emerging new generation of lay and married Catholic theologians, the most competent and knowledgeable author on the history and function of the theological magisterium and the issues and challenges it faces in the church today.

INTRODUCTION

In this volume, Robert Nugent writes eloquently of the troubles that four major twentieth-century Catholic thinkers had with church authorities. He offers us moving yet painful testimonies of the ways in which these figures often felt hounded and betrayed by the church to which they had dedicated their lives. Each was haunted by accusations that they were departing from "the unchangeable doctrine of the church." These accusations could only make sense, however, within a particular ecclesiological framework. That framework began to take shape with the rise of ultramontanism in the early nineteenth century and came into full bloom in the first half of the twentieth century, in which these four theologians lived. This framework reduced the great tradition of the church to a monochromatic scholasticism, authentic leadership to ecclesiastical paternalism, and the personal response of believers to an unthinking canonical obedience. How this situation came to be is too long a story for these few pages. In the nineteenth century, we began to see a new framework for the relationship between theologians and those holding apostolic office. Over the course of little more than a century from Pope Gregory XVI to Pope Pius XII, the papacy was transformed from the doctrinal court of final appeal to the supreme doctrinal watchdog vigilant to snuff out any sign of theological innovation. It is easy for us to forget that it was not always thus.

Consider, if you will, the sixteenth and seventeenth century *de auxiliis* ["regarding the divine helps"] controversy between the Jesuits and the Dominicans regarding the relationship between divine grace and human freedom. The papacy inserted itself into the controversy only after the two religious orders had begun accusing each other of harboring heretical views. Papal investigations began under Pope Clement VIII but came to their conclusion two papacies later, under Pope Paul V. The papal investigation included the conduct of seventeen debates between representatives of the principal theological positions. Finally, Paul V resolved the matter by way of a decree that prohibited either side from condemning the views of the other, with the pope reminding each side that they were delving into nothing less than the holy mystery of God. This papal act implicitly acknowledged the difficult and speculative theological issues being considered. Horrific stories, familiar to many, of the abuses of the inquisition should prevent us from romanticizing the premodern era of the church, but there can be no denying the quantitative increase in papal interventions in theological debates from the nineteenth century onward.

By the first half of the twentieth century, sad stories such as those of Teilhard, Congar, Murray, and Merton were common and gave evidence of an ecclesiastical authority far too willing to snuff out legitimate theological inquiry and investigation. Pope Pius XII, in his 1950 encyclical *Humani Generis*, seemed to limit the vocation of the theologian to that of faithfully explicating that which was proclaimed by the pope and bishops. Theologians were teachers of the faith only by virtue of a delegation of authority from the bishops. They were expected to submit their work to the authoritative scrutiny and potential censorship of the magisterium. "Dissent," understood as the rejection or even questioning of any authoritative teaching of the magisterium, was viewed with suspicion as an attack on the authority of the magisterium itself.

Of course, this was not absolute. The dogmatic manuals acknowledged the legitimacy of limited speculative discussion that was critical of certain doctrinal formulations. Moreover, the manual tradition also incorporated a sophisticated taxonomy of church teaching known as the "theological notes." Theological notes were formal judgments by theologians or the magisterium on the precise relationship of a doctrinal formulation to divine revelation. Their purpose was to safeguard the faith and prevent confusion between binding doctrines and theological opinion. Within this neo-scholastic framework, the assumption was that if theologians discovered a significant difficulty with a doctrinal formulation that had not been proposed infallibly, they were to bring the difficulty to the attention of the hierarchy in private and to refrain from any public speech or writing that was contrary to received church teaching. Sadly, the postconciliar instruction by the Congregation for the Doctrine of the Faith (CDF) *On the Ecclesial Vocation of the Theologian* insisted upon these same constraints.[1]

The Second Vatican Council offered a potentially new framework for understanding the relationship between the church's teaching office and the vocation of the theologian. Gone was the "trickle-down" theory of divine revelation, conceived as a collection of propositional truths transmitted exclusively to the bishops. In its place was a theology of revelation that began with the trinitarian self-communication of God in the person of Jesus Christ. According to the council's Dogmatic Constitution on Divine Revelation (*Dei*

Verbum, no. 10), this revelation was given to the whole church and not just the bishops. The bishops would remain the authoritative guardians of that revelation by virtue of their apostolic office. However, the Word of God resided in the whole church as each of the baptized was given a supernatural instinct for the faith that allowed them to recognize God's Word, penetrate its meaning more deeply and apply it more profoundly in their lives (*Lumen Gentium* no. 12; *Dei Verbum*, no. 8).

The council did not reflect explicitly on the role of the theologian in any depth. However, several passages are worth considering. The council insisted that the work of biblical exegesis and theology must be done under the guidance of the magisterium: "Catholic exegetes…and other students of sacred theology, working diligently together and using appropriate means, should devote their energies, under the watchful care of the sacred teaching office of the Church, to an exploration and exposition of the divine writings" (*Dei Verbum*, no. 23).

They reiterated that it was the responsibility of theologians to interpret and explicate church teaching faithfully. However, these tasks did not exhaust the work of theologians. Theologians must also consider new questions:

> …recent research and discoveries in the sciences, in history and philosophy bring up new problems which have an important bearing on life itself and demand new scrutiny by theologians. Furthermore, theologians are now being asked, within the methods and limits of theological science, to develop more efficient ways of communicating doctrine to the people of today (*Gaudium et Spes*, no. 64).

In several other texts, the bishops encouraged theologians to explore unresolved doctrinal questions (*Lumen Gentium*, no. 54). The council's very decrees gave evidence of a legitimate development of doctrine, a development fueled by the unique contributions of theologians such as Congar and Murray.

The decades immediately after the council held promise for a new framework for considering the relationship between the magisterium and the theologian. Pope Paul VI, for example, created the International Theological Commission as a way of formalizing a positive and constructive relationship between the church's teaching office and the theological community. Unfortunately, this commission was placed under the presidency of the prefect for the Congregation for the Doctrine of the Faith (CDF) and, over the course of the first decades of its existence, curial pressure led to the exclusion from its membership of important voices that were at times critical of certain church pronouncements.

In the pontificate of John Paul II, the promulgation of the "Profession of Faith and Oath of Fidelity" (1989), the Vatican instruction, "On the Ecclesial Vocation of the Theologian" (1990) and the papal letter, *Ad Tuendam Fidem* (For the Defense of the Faith, 1998), were all oriented toward limiting the theologian's freedom to critically assess even church teachings that had not been proposed infallibly. In 1997, new procedures were introduced for the investigation of theologians by the CDF, purportedly to better protect the rights of the theologian being investigated. For example, the local bishop of the theologian being investigated plays a much greater role in the process and the theologian being investigated may now draw on the assistance of a theological advisor of his or her choosing. Yet, many of the abuses of authority evident in the ways in which Teilhard, Congar,

Murray, and Merton were treated have continued. Theologians who have endured Vatican investigations in the decades since the council complain that they are never allowed to confront their accuser and that there is a veil of secrecy imposed on the proceedings, thereby inhibiting transparency. These investigations often presume guilt rather than innocence and interpret the theologian's work in a remarkably uncontextualized fashion. Such investigations rarely take into account the gradation of levels of doctrinal authority. According to the Vatican's instruction "On the Theological Vocation of the Theologian," there are four different levels of church teaching:

1. dogma—teachings that are proposed infallibly as divinely revealed (e.g., the divinity of Christ);
2. definitive doctrine—teachings that are proposed infallibly which, although not divinely revealed are necessary to safeguard and defend divine revelation (e.g., the Council of Trent's determination of the books that were in the biblical canon);
3. authoritative doctrine—teachings that are drawn from the church's ongoing reflection on divine revelation but which are not divinely revealed and are not taught infallibly (e.g., the prohibition of recourse to artificial contraception);
4. church discipline (e.g., canon law prohibiting married men to be ordained to the presbyterate in the Latin rite).

In spite of this carefully developed set of distinctions in church teaching, in the current ecclesiastical climate a theological challenge to a teaching that has the status of authoritative doctrine is often treated the same as a repudiation of church dogma.

Over four decades removed from the close of the Second Vatican Council, we are still waiting for a new framework to emerge for conceiving the relationship between the magisterium and theologians, one informed by the theological trajectories introduced at the council. Such a paradigm would begin with the recognition that the ministry of theologians shares with the ministry of the bishops a common commitment to the Word of God even if the principal responsibility of the bishops is to safeguard the integrity of the apostolic faith (*Dei Verbum*, no. 10). This means that the magisterium is, by definition, conservative. I do not use the word *conservative* here in its ideological sense (conservative as opposed to liberal), but in its most fundamental meaning. As Francis Sullivan has observed, "...its [the magisterium's] primary function is not to penetrate into the depths of the mysteries of faith (the task of theology) but rather to safeguard the priceless treasure of the word of God and to defend the purity of the faith of the Christian community."[2]

The work of the theological community is, by its nature, more tentative and experimental than that of the bishops. It is oriented toward (1) deepening the church's ongoing reception of the faith and (2) raising new questions and illuminating new contexts for the dynamic reception of the faith. Given the inherently provisional and experimental character of most theological reflection, when a theologian publishes a work, the assumption ought not to be that she is offering the final word on a topic, but that she is offering a fresh theological investigation to the theological community for its assessment. Anyone who has attended a serious theological conference knows that the community of theologians takes this responsibility very seriously. Major theological contributions are invariably subject to intense academic scrutiny. The best theologians welcome the critical conversation that ensues upon the publication of their views, seeing each publication, not as a definitive pronouncement, but as the contribution toward a larger work in progress. Those who argue that the magisterium has an obligation to take an aggressive, interventionist stance in policing the work of theologians overlook the effective way in which the theological community assesses its own productions. A few years ago, at an annual convention of the Catholic Theological Society of America, I attended a session in which a noted and somewhat controversial theologian gave a lively response to over thirty critical peer reviews of his new book!

Frequently, when a theologian makes a new contribution to his field, the critical give-and-take among his fellow scholars revolves around the fruitfulness of the particular line of inquiry explored in the work. Scholars might criticize the interpretation of historical data or the methodology employed. Occasionally theologians will find it necessary to make their own judgments regarding the coherence of a particular theological work with the official teaching of the church. They do so with the honest recognition that all theological reflection falls short in some decisive way in the face of the incomprehensible mystery of God.

One sometimes hears the complaint that Catholic theologians today present themselves as a "competing magisterium" to that of the college of bishops. This caricature gains credence more by its widespread repetition than by any objective analysis of the situation in the church today. I personally know of no serious Catholic theologian who holds that they possess the same authority as that of the college of bishops. Indeed, in my experience the vast majority of Catholic theologians recognize the unique role that the bishops play in the life of the church. They acknowledge a legitimate accountability to the ecclesiastical magisterium even as they may disagree with the concrete manner in which ecclesiastical oversight may be exercised.

I suspect that the dangers posed by "dissenting" theologians have been exaggerated. Credentialed Catholic theologians are readily identified, and to the extent that they speak in public or publish their views, they are easily held accountable for their fidelity to the great tradition of the church. If a particular theologian proposes a position clearly at variance with church teaching, the church's teaching office should make a straightforward statement to the effect that position X proposed by theologian Y does not, at present, represent the accepted teaching of the church. This it does in order to assist those who, lacking scholarly expertise, might be misled or confused regarding the status of a given theological perspective. A number of years ago, the archbishop of Milwaukee, Rembert Weakland, made a public declaration that the views of a particular theologian in his diocese on the morality of abortion did not represent the teaching of the Catholic Church. However, it is quite another thing to brand a scholar indiscriminately as a "dissenting theologian." A theologian might in the course of her work offer a particular viewpoint on a certain issue that, in the judgment of the magisterium, is not in full accord with official church teaching. This hardly means that everything that theologian writes or says must be held suspect.

The following proposals seem worthy of consideration as the church today seeks a new framework for conceiving magisterium-theologian relationship:

First, doctrinal investigations should honor the historical context of all church teaching. Much theological work is oriented toward interpreting church doctrine in its historical context and recognizing the need for a legitimate development. What may appear superficially as a departure from church teaching in fact may better be apprehended as a necessary recontextualization of that teaching.

Second, the exercise of the church's teaching office must be more cognizant of the theological significance of the gradation of authority in church teachings. Too often one encounters a form of "creeping infallibility" that levels out all church teachings and fails to recognize that those proposed authoritatively but not definitively are intrinsically provisional and open to theological disputation.

Third, disciplinary investigations of the work of theologians should honor the distinction between doctrine and theology. It is the task of the magisterium to safeguard the doctrinal integrity of the apostolic faith. This means that the bishops are duty bound to speak out where they encounter a clear and substantive departure from a core teaching of the church. However, too many recent disciplinary decrees censure, not clear and obvious departures from the great tradition of the church, but rather what are presented as "troubling," "potentially misleading" or "confusing" doctrinal interpretations found in the works of certain theologians. The complaint, in other words, is not so much one of evident doctrinal deviation, as of a discomfort with a theological approach or emphasis. The magisterium is to be the authoritative arbiter of doctrinal integrity not theological adequacy. The latter task falls to the theological community itself.

Fourth, when the magisterium finds it necessary to investigate, pass judgment and, in rare and extraordinary circumstances, impose sanctions on the work of a theologian it should draw on a much greater diversity of expert opinions. At present, the consulters employed by the CDF are drawn

Introduction

overwhelmingly from Roman universities representing a narrow ideological band of theological opinion.

Fifth, the procedures for investigating theologians must be thoroughly revised in order to ensure the dignity and preserve the good reputation of the theologian being investigated. This demands complete transparency at every point of the process, the right of the theologian to know what party has raised a complaint, the free access of all parties to all of the relevant documents pertaining to the case, and the cultivation of a climate of dialogue rather than adversarial interrogation. Such a procedure was developed by the U.S. bishops in consultation with both the Catholic Theological Society of America and the Canon Law Society of America in the document, *Shared Doctrinal Responsibilities*. Sadly, the helpful procedures outlined in the document have rarely been employed.

As the reader engages Nugent's lucid and inspiring accounts of the travails of Teilhard, Congar, Murray, and Merton, it will be difficult to ignore the fact that in spite of the many advances and contributions of the Second Vatican Council, so much of the inquisitorial atmosphere in which they lived is still present in the church today. It is my fervent hope that by giving greater prominence to these four figures, this volume will contribute to the exploration of a new framework for conceiving the relationship between the magisterium and theologians, a framework more in keeping with a community of Jesus' disciples.

Richard Gaillardetz
Murray/Beck Professor of Catholic Studies
University of Toledo in Ohio

11

Chapter One

TEILHARD DE CHARDIN AND THE HOLY OFFICE

Introduction

On November 13, 1924, a relatively unknown Jesuit scientist, Pierre Teilhard de Chardin, received a letter from his religious superior summoning him to a meeting in Lyon, France. The meeting was the beginning of difficulties with ecclesiastical authorities that would end only with Teilhard's death in 1955. For the rest of his life he would shuttle back and forth between France, China, and the United States for field research, teaching, and lectures. Often the trips outside France were the result of decisions of his own Jesuit superiors in order to protect him. At other times, his banishment was imposed by Roman authorities troubled by the impact of his novel theological views on original sin and evolution for traditional church doctrines and his increasing influence in theological circles.

Early Years

Teilhard de Chardin was born on May 1, 1881, on the family estate of Saracenat in the province of Auvergne. He entered the Jesuit novitiate at Aix-en-Provence in 1899 that was later relocated to Paris and then to the Isle of Jersey after religious orders were expelled from France.

In 1905, he began his teaching internship in physics and chemistry at the Jesuit College of the Holy Family in Cairo, Egypt. After three years, he returned to Europe to complete theological studies at Ore Place in Hastings, England, from 1908 to 1912. He was ordained a priest on August 24, 1911, at the age of thirty.

From 1912 to 1915, he studied paleontology in Paris, took part in several archeological digs, and contributed articles to professional journals. His studies and research were interrupted by World War I during which he served as a stretcher-bearer with the Eighth Regiment of the Moroccan riflemen, known as the North African Zouaves. For this service, he was awarded France's Legion of Honor in 1921. In 1922, he earned a doctorate in science at the Sorbonne.

An Atmosphere of Fear

As early as 1914, when he returned from his duties as stretcher-bearer, he spoke of the witch-hunts and denunciations of theologians suspected of Modernism, then underway in the church: "Out of all that has been attempted during the past twenty years to defend religion in our country, nothing and nobody has been spared."[1]

In 1903, Pius X (1903–1914), who orchestrated a widespread campaign to combat a variety of supposed dangerous theological trends lumped under the title "Modernism," was elected to succeed a more progressive pope, Leo XIII (1878–1903). One of the new pope's most effective weapons in his battle against Modernism was to put certain authors on the Index of Forbidden Books. In 1904, the French philosopher Henri Bergson (1859–1941), one of the first to

integrate evolutionary theology into his thought, was condemned by the Holy Office and his writings put on the
Index. As a student, Teilhard had read and admired Bergson,
and years later, he would be offered a teaching position at
the College de France where Bergson himself had taught. In
Teilhard's view, Bergson was "a kind of saint."[2]

Ten years later while in China on a scientific expedition,
Teilhard wrote to friends that he had depressing news from
Paris about the growing influence of the integrist movement.
The movement was an effort by some influential people in
the church to preserve the integrity of church doctrines in
opposition to "Modernists" who championed critical schol-
arship in the theological and biblical sciences. He decided to
limit his own writings to the domain of disputable scientific
facts, although he said, "no force on earth would make him
modify the direction or intensity" of the influence he could
bring to bear in other disciplines.[3] Sensing, perhaps, some of
the problems he would eventually have to face himself, he
added that he hoped he could be preserved from any bitter-
ness and be able to see that God's activity can be found
"even in the most disagreeable maneuvers of various obtuse
or pharisaical minds."[4] Shortly thereafter his resolution
would be put to the test. Not only would his orthodoxy, loyalty, and patience be sorely tried repeatedly through the
coming years, but also his very faith in the church itself
would be questioned by the continual opposition of ecclesiastical authorities to his work.

By the fall of 1922, he was lecturing at the Institut
Catholique and was already known to be a promoter of the
developing theory of evolution. The death of Pius X in 1914
virtually ended the campaign, which had employed a semi-
secret organization to spy on and report certain theologians,
to eliminate so-called Modernists. However, the new pope,

Silence Speaks

Benedict XV (1914–1922), began a similar campaign against the "new theology," including dangerous theories of evolution and other theological ideas and trends emanating from France that upset Vatican officials.

Under Suspicion

The 1924 meeting in Lyon, noted above, came about because of a paper Teilhard had written a few years earlier on some tentative approaches to a new interpretation of the doctrine of original sin. The essay mysteriously found its way to Rome. One theory is that a student at the Institut Catholique, anxious to prove his own orthodoxy to church authorities, stole the document from Teilhard's room. The essay came to the attention of the Spanish cardinal Rafael Merry del Val (1865–1930), who had been the charismatic and powerful secretary of state under Pius X and one of the leading exponents of the anti-Modernist crusade. Teilhard's Jesuit superior general, Wladimir Ledochowski, had been warned previously about growing suspicions in Rome about Teilhard. Ledochowski was a former Austrian military official and a favorite of the conservative party in Rome. Pope Pius XII later tapped him to head a committee charged with drafting an encyclical condemning Nazism that was written but never made public.

The Holy Office asked Teilhard to promise in writing that he would "never say anything against the traditional position of the Church on original sin."[5] He felt the demand was both too vague and too absolute. He had, he believed, the right to carry on scientific research with other professionals and to bring help to those in the church who were disturbed and troubled by some of the official formulations of traditional church doctrine. In place of the proffered Roman wording, he suggested an alternative. He would promise, he said, "not to spread (not to carry on proselytism) for the particular explanations contained in my note."[6] His Jesuit superiors and the rector of the Institut Catholique tried to work out a more amenable solution, but Rome would have none of it. In the end, he was forced to subscribe to six propositions, of which only one caused him any serious difficulty. On the advice of his friends, he reluctantly signed the document on July 25, 1925, though not before giving some serious thought to doing so with mental reservations. His license to teach at the Institut was permanently revoked.

Teilhard's initial reaction to the ban was seemingly one of total faith: "At heart I am at perfect peace. Even this is a manifestation of Our Lord and one of his operations. So why worry."[7] Nevertheless, the action had affected him more profoundly perhaps than he realized. Only a year later he confessed to a friend that what he felt inside was something like a death agony or a storm. Some colleagues suggested he consider leaving the Jesuit Order and the church so he could work more freely as a scientist. He rejected that advice and later in life said he had never really been tempted to leave because if he did, "People would think that I was straying from the Church; I should be accused of pride. I must show by my example that if my ideas appear in the light of an innovation, they make me as faithful as anyone else to the attitude in which I was formerly seen. That is how it seems to me—But even now, the shadows fall."[8]

The shadows would continue to fall for the rest of his life, causing great personal suffering and serious conflicts of conscience. He was also compelled to withdraw from his teaching position at the Institut Catholique and confined himself to scientific research while keeping theological speculation to himself. By the end of the year, he was still reflecting on the whole experience and reaffirming his faith in the order and the church. He reasoned that leaving either would be an undisciplined act that would have caused enormous damage and scandal: "Nothing spiritual or divine can come to a Christian or to one who has taken religious vows, except through the Church or his Order....I believe in the Church as the mediator between God and the world and I love it....But I don't yet see the reforms which are desirable."[9]

Struggles with Faith and Church

In 1926, either at his own request or, some claim, that of his superiors, he was sent to China, no doubt to put both geographical and psychological distance between himself and the growing atmosphere of suspicions and sanctions in the church. He would remain there, on and off, for the next twenty years, settling in Beijing from 1926–1935, and traveling freely to many other parts of the world for research and lectures. The next four years were crucial ones during which he experienced the depths of the struggle between faith in the church and the temptation to abandon both church and priesthood, although he claimed later in life that he was never seriously tempted in these directions. Still chafing at the narrowness of some official Catholic views, he wrote to a friend, "We are no longer 'Catholic' in fact; but we are defending a system, a sect."[10] He also said,

In a kind of way I no longer have confidence in the exterior manifestations of the Church. I believe that through it the divine influence will continue to reach me, but I no longer have much belief in the immediate and tangible value of official directions and decisions. Some people feel happy in the visible Church; but for my own part I think I shall be happy to die in order to be free of it—and to find our Lord outside of it.[11]

Many years later, however, he confided to a friend that he was never tempted to free himself from the church or his order. Perhaps the freedom for which he was searching would only finally come through death.

His friends undertook efforts to have him return to his teaching post, but these were unsuccessful. A colleague once reminded him that the Society of Jesus was not an order of pioneers. Teilhard strongly disagreed but said he had no intention of leaving and would even be willing to soften his ideas to make them more acceptable. He realized his obedience would not come without a cost. He would drink from the chalice with deep joy, he said, knowing that he drank the Blood of Christ and yet "I swallow the obstacle in the act of my obedience."[12]

During this period, he wrote one of his most popular books, *The Divine Milieu*. He was also working on an article titled "The Phenomenon of Man" for the French journal *Scientia* that later became a book by the same title. Neither of these works was published during his lifetime, although as manuscripts both were widely circulated in scientific and theological circles. In order to avoid further complications, he often employed a pseudonym to publish smaller articles in professional journals. The fact that his more visionary writings were never subject to public criticism by his peers is probably one of the chief reasons for many of the problems he encountered with church authorities during his lifetime.

In China, out of the French Catholic culture and somewhat removed from ecclesiastical authorities, he had some distance to reflect on his situation. In the winter of 1927–28, he confessed to an acute crisis of anti-ecclesiasticism, if not anti-Christianity. He found his only consolation in his practice of believing in the Spirit:

> ...it would be very unjust to regard the Church as the one place where the spirit is not found. I begin to think that most of our weaknesses are due to the fact that our belief is too narrow, and that we don't believe through the end. To stop believing a second too soon, or not to believe enough is sufficient to ruin the whole structure of what we are building.[13]

Early in 1929, Teilhard learned that the Jesuit censors in Louvain were very favorable to *The Divine Milieu* and that it was on the point of being printed. Still, he worried: "...everything depends on how my official relations with Rome develop; and I'm very much afraid that I'll never manage to regain a clean slate in that quarter."[14] However, in the depths of his heart, he was more hopeful. He had passed, he thought, a turning point, a critical juncture in his intellectual and emotional life without a break and had become an adult in terms of his relationship with the Jesuit Order: "...unless ...I found myself forced into some intellectual dishonesty, I am determined to remain faithful to it whatever the cost."[15] The cost would be high.

By December 1929, there was still no word about *The Divine Milieu*, which was to have been published that past July. He speculated that some flaw had been found in the work and described it as more of the same negative criticism and vague nominalism characteristic of Roman authorities. At the same time, the diocesan censors in Malines, Belgium, stopped another article on "transformism" from publication in that country. His frustration erupted privately in a letter to a friend:

…this tenacious and persistent obstructionism is infinitely wearing…the only thing that I can be: a voice that repeats…that the Church will waste away so long as she does not escape from the fictitious world of verbal theology, of quantitative sacramentalism, and over-refined devotions in which she is enveloped, so as to reincarnate herself in the real aspirations of mankind.[16]

He was keenly aware of the paradox of his situation. If he needed Christ and the church, he reasoned, he should also accept the burden of rites, administration, and theology: "But now I can't get away from the evidence that the moment has come when the Christian impulse should 'save Christ' from the hands of the clerics so that the world may be saved."[17] At this point, the tensions around the issue of his relationship with the order and the church seemed to have taken on a more peaceful tone.

He advised Leontine Zanata, a lifelong friend and confidant, never to "let go of these two threads of loyalty towards ourselves and attachment to the Church….Pray that I may never break either of them."[18] He must have been tempted to do just that many times despite his protestations to the contrary.

The suspicions that plagued his professional efforts, ideas, and writings continued to cause him stress. Those who offered support were often unable to empathize with his unique situation as a scientist and believer. On one occasion, a superior, surely in good faith, told him precisely what the attitude of a Catholic scientist should be: "The Catholic scientist has an infallible rule which spares him many wasted labors: he must dismiss *a priori* all that contradicts Catholic dogma."[19] One can only imagine Teilhard's reaction to such advice!

A Stubborn Son of the Church

Despite the suspicion, restrictions, rejections, and prohibitions, Teilhard strove to live faithfully his vow of obedience. He would not publish without an imprimatur. He argued his case as strongly as possible in private correspondence to professionals, friends, and supporters, but never publicly. Abbé Paul Grenet, a close friend, described Teilhard as an obedient but stubborn son of the church. A Jesuit colleague, Père d'Quince, said that Teilhard's religious superiors could always count on his obedience and docility, but at the same time "he never left them in any doubt of whatever he thought unduly rigorous in their decisions, and right up to the end...he asked for a revision of a policy of prudence which seemed contrary both to his own interior vocation and to the interests of the Church."[20]

By February 1931, he had completed the final revision of *The Divine Milieu*, but Jesuit censors at Louvain suggested additional changes, which he readily made. At Christmas, he was told that even further precision was required, especially where he had written about the cross, grace, and the role of the supernatural. Once again, he complied willingly.

In 1932, Teilhard was living again in a Jesuit community and had returned to what he called a "semi-religious life," although he acknowledged that the lay milieu was his natural milieu. He accepted the minimal ecclesiastical framework in which he found himself, but said he did not take it seriously enough any longer for it to cause him deep suffering: "And then I keep telling myself that if I were less deeply inserted within the Church, I would be less equipped for the work of setting her free."[21]

The ecclesiastical framework, however, continued to be a source of irritation if not personal suffering. Roman theologians were studying an unrevised manuscript of *The Divine Milieu* that had somehow found its way to Rome. As a result, hopes for imminent publication were dashed once again. The book was eventually published only in 1957—two years after his death and still without an imprimatur.

Continuing Restrictions

During the winter of 1934, complaints about Teilhard continued to find their way to Rome. He toyed with the idea of going to Rome personally to talk with church authorities and to explain his views: "It's tiresome," he complained "that they make no attempt in Rome to see what is constructive in my effort."[22] His Jesuit superior in Lyon advised against the visit, so Teilhard abandoned the idea. How, he wondered, could he make an honorable peace when he knew they had a "loaded dossier" against him? Two years later, he was again considering a visit to Rome, but only if he could go without a rope around his neck. He wanted to try to make them see in Rome what he saw, but this was not to be and his dossier in Rome was growing.

From 1939 until 1946, Teilhard was trapped in China because of World War II. When he returned to France, he was already a well-known and influential thinker because of the informal distribution of his manuscripts, especially through the French resistance.

In 1940, he was invited to attend a scientific congress in New York, but Rome forbade his participation. They would have been happier, he mused in one of his more playful moods, if he had announced the inauguration of a new pilgrimage.

By June 1941, Teilhard had completed yet another revision demanded by Rome of *The Phenomenon of Man*, in the hope of seeing its publication. In 1944, he was informed that the Roman censors had found it unacceptable and had forbidden its publication. In 1946, Father Reginald Garrigou-Legrange, a Dominican theologian in his own right and an official of the Holy Office, criticized him in an article that appeared in *L'Osservatore Romano*.

The Vatican was growing increasingly uneasy with what some in Rome disparagingly called the "new theology" emanating from France and decided to undertake a crackdown. As a result, Rome ordered a total ban on the French worker-priest experiment that the Cardinal Archbishop of Paris had initiated and supported. Teilhard had supported the experiment and took the decision very hard.

In order to protect him, his superiors asked him not to write any more philosophy. He agreed to this further "interior submission to the Church," though psychologically he found it very difficult. Naively, it seems, he thought the Holy Office's ban was simply a matter of misunderstanding on their part that could and would eventually be cleared up. In the meantime, he continued to press his case with his own superiors.

When confronted with charges that Teilhard was a pantheistic heretic, Archbishop Angelo Roncalli, then the papal nuncio in Paris, pushed them aside: "This Teilhard fellow...why can't he be content with the catechism and the social doctrine of the Church, instead of bringing up all these problems?"[23] Later as Pope John XXIII, he was more tolerant of modern theologians because he believed that in France new ideas were born with wings and that without a touch of holy madness, the church could not grow.

Teilhard argued his case to the new Jesuit Superior General, John Baptist Janssens, that all of the written accusations against him predated 1939 and were based on writings that had been circulating unofficially. Now that he had time to refine his thinking he reminded Janssens that respected theologians had followed his thought and had judged that he had made progress toward an orthodox explanation of his views: "Don't you think," he asked, "it would be a pity to reject without examination a fruit which is perhaps on the point of ripening?"[24]

In October 1948, Janssens finally invited him to visit Rome where Teilhard had hoped to accomplish several things. He had been nominated for a professorship in prehistory at the prestigious College of France and wanted permission to accept the honor. He also wanted the imprimatur for the publication of *The Phenomenon of Man* that had been denied in 1944. Finally, he wanted to have the ban on his teaching lifted. None of these were accomplished during the visit.

He arrived in Rome at midnight, October 4–5, and was met at the train station by one of his many friends. He was housed in the section of the Jesuit headquarters reserved for visiting dignitaries and was won over immediately by the honest, direct, and human approach of his Jesuit general.

Teilhard's recorded reaction to the paradox of Rome and St. Peter's, in particular, is in keeping with his evolutionary vision of life and the world. He felt that the "humbling assurance [of St. Peter's] representing the earthly extremity of an arc springing out between man and what is beyond man—the great affair beside which the inflated baroque of the churches, and the penitential wands in the confessionals, and the most bewildering display of ecclesiastical accouterments that you can imagine all disappear."[25]

An amusing incident occurred when Teilhard encountered the Cardinal Ratzinger of his day, the Dominican Garrigou-Lagrange, his principle adversary at the Holy Office. "There is the man," Teilhard is reported to have said to a companion at a Roman reception attended by both he and Garrigou-Lagrange, "who would like to see me burnt at the stake."²⁶ According to Teilhard's version, when they were introduced they smiled amicably and talked pleasantly of Auvergne, a section in France, from which they both had come.

During his visit to Rome, Teilhard was unable to see Pius XII, who was vacationing at Castel Gondolfo. The pope, however, was aware of Teilhard's work and made his own judgment. After hearing of his scientific research in China, Pius is reported to have responded that although Teilhard was a great scientist, he was not a theologian. In one of his essays, the pope said, "he speaks of resolving the 'problem of God.' But for us there is no problem."²⁷ Pius also told a French politician that while he was on the papal throne, Teilhard would never be condemned. The pope kept his word.

Teilhard returned from Rome obviously disappointed but nonetheless determined to continue with his work. He even found ways to circumvent some of the limitations. To the English Jesuit author, C. C. Martindale, to whom he sent some pamphlets, he said that he thought the work was orthodox and "you will know how to make discreet use of it. The people up high are not so keen on my circulating these things, and after all one must preserve a little obedience."²⁸

Exile and Last Days

In 1950 Pius XII published the encyclical *Humani Generis*, which some commentators believe contains an implicit rebuke of Teilhard's theory of evolution. The encyclical condemned the acceptance of polygenism and any changes in the church's teaching on original sin. Progressive thinkers in the church were discouraged by the tone of the encyclical. Teilhard tried to console them privately, telling them that for an encyclical thus titled, it would be difficult to present a narrower view of humanity. He described it as a kind of sadism and masochism of an orthodoxy that forces people to swallow truth under crude and stupid forms. For himself, he planned to continue quite simply along his own way in a direction that Rome wanted. The public controversy and lively debate that the encyclical generated in the church affected Teilhard personally, although not directly, in terms of any further intensification of the official restrictions already imposed upon him.

In the aftermath of public reactions to the new encyclical, he judged that the press was speaking too much about him and his supposed indiscretions. Things were getting "too hot" for him and he thought it best to disappear for a time. He was becoming, he thought, an embarrassment to church authorities and felt it might be better to give Rome the impression that he was delving back into what Roman authorities called "pure science."

Teilhard headed back to New York, stopping along the way in South Africa, Buenos Aires, and Rio de Janeiro. Ironically, despite the continued restrictions and prohibitions and the personal pain of his forced exile, he was able to declare in 1951 that he felt himself to be more bound to the church than he had ever been. In the same year, however, fearing that his work would not be published even after his death, he willed all rights to his nonscientific writing to his literary executrix, Jeanne Mortier.

This peaceful resignation and personal act of faith would serve him well in the difficulties that were far from over. In 1954, he was given permission for a three-month return visit to France, beginning on June 3, a visit that was to be his last. At the end of July, in Paris, he received word from Rome that his request to publish a response to an article published by the prominent critic of the church and noted scientist Jean Rostand had been denied. In addition, he was ordered to return to New York as soon as possible. By an ironic and painful coincidence, he received the harsh news on July 31, the patronal feast of Saint Ignatius of Loyola, the founder of the Society of Jesus.

During Teilhard's lifetime, few people realized the extent of the emotional toll these experiences took on his spirit. He continued to suffer from constant misunderstanding and mistrust by church authorities until the last years of his life. After his death, a close friend revealed something of what this entailed:

> He bore with patience, it is true, trials that might well have proved too much for the strongest of us, but how often in intimate conversation have I found him depressed and with almost no heart to carry on. The agonizing distress he already had to face in 1939 was intensified in the following years, and he sometimes felt that he could venture no further. During that period he was at times prostrated by fits of weeping and he appeared to be on the verge of despair. But calling on all the resources of his will, he abandoned himself to…Christ as the only purpose of his being; and so hid his suffering and took up his work again, if not with joy, at least in the hope that his personal vocation might be fulfilled.[29]

The intransigence of Rome continued to plague him even during his last relatively peaceful few years in New York. In 1955, he was invited to participate in a paleontological symposium sponsored by the Sorbonne in Paris. When Rome learned of it, they wrote to forbid his participation. In another intervention, Rome put a stop to a project instigated by his

Jesuit friends in Louvain to have a German translation of some of his articles made by the Benziger Publishing Company. At times, resistance to his thought from church authorities seemed to energize him because he felt very sure that what he was saying was really the same thing in the minds of many other people in the church.

On Easter Sunday 1952, Teilhard went to New York's St. Patrick's Cathedral to hear the renowned preacher Fulton Sheen. He recorded his response to Sheen, whom he saw as a splendid orator. However, he seems to have concluded that Sheen oversimplified life to a certain extent, glossing over complexities that, for Teilhard, were part of the very mystery of creation.

Part of the Teilhard legend recounts how he is supposed to have told a friend a few days before his death: "If in my life I haven't been wrong, I beg God to allow me to die on Easter Sunday." He died of heart failure on Easter Sunday, April 10, 1955, at six o'clock in the evening. The funeral Mass was held at St. Ignatius parish with a few friends in attendance. The body was then taken to the Jesuit novitiate of St.-Andrews-on-the-Hudson, Poughkeepsie, in upstate New York, where it remains today, although the novitiate was subsequently relocated and the property subsequently purchased by the Culinary Institute of America.

Between 1955 and 1973, Teilhard's works, including *The Divine Milieu* and *The Phenomenon of Man*, were published in France and quickly translated into English. But even in death he was not free from ecclesiastical suspicion and posthumous Church censorship. On June 30, 1962, just four months before the opening of Vatican II, the Holy Office published a *monitum* warning people against his writings. The most eminent and reverend fathers of the Holy Office wrote to seminaries, religious houses, and universities about

Teilhard's ambiguities and serious errors especially in order to protect youth against the dangers of Teilhard de Chardin.

Peter Hebblethwaite claims that John XXIII never actually read Teilhard and so was not in a position to judge the *monitum*: "But, strangely enough, 'Chardanian' phrases began to enter the speeches he was working on at the time. The optimism of his inaugural address to the Council, his fascination with space travel which allowed the world to be seen as 'one planet,' and his references to 'a new order of human relationships' all echoed Teilhardian themes."[30]

Although Teilhard de Chardin was dead, his spirit and name were very much alive at Vatican II. Cardinal Frings of Cologne created an uproar in the council hall when he openly criticized the Holy Office for methods that did not conform to the modern era and scandalized the world. Paul VI reportedly telephoned Frings to express his approval.

At the third session in 1964, South Africa's Archbishop Hurley spoke approvingly of Teilhard's splendid vision as religious, scientific, evolutionary, and eschatological. In even stronger terms, Archbishop D'Souza of Bhopal, India, responding to the misgivings, cautions, warnings, and criticisms voiced by some council fathers against schema 13, raised the specter of the Galileo affair and compared the treatment of Teilhard with that of the church's response to Lamennais, Darwin, Marx, and Freud. He suggested that while their works were not without error, they were nonetheless in tune with the schema and yet still they were indiscriminately condemned. A German bishop regretted "the censuring of Pierre Teilhard de Chardin, a devout priest respected by scientists. The Church does not seem to be learning the lessons of the Galileo case."[31]

When the council documents were published, several commentators claimed to have found significant traces of Teilhard's positive, evolutionary view of the world in some

---

of them, including the Pastoral Constitution on the Church in the Modern World, which acknowledged: "The destiny of the human race is viewed as a complete whole, no longer, as it were, in the particular histories of various peoples: now it merges into a complete whole. And so humankind substitutes a dynamic and more evolutionary concept of nature for a static one."[32]

A friend once asked Teilhard if he did not find some consolation in seeing the growing influence of his teaching on others. He replied that his work would only be fulfilled when others went beyond him. As for the intransigence of church authorities, he tried to meet it with serenity—and, at times, with a sense of humor: "I am prepared to go on," he once said, "and with a smile if possible."[33]

On the centennial birthday anniversary of Pierre Teilhard de Chardin, celebrated in Paris at the Institut Catholique, Agostino Casaroli, the Vatican Secretary of State, sent a letter on behalf of John Paul II dated June 10, 1981, to Archbishop Paul Poupard, the rector of the university.

The letter described Teilhard as a man possessed by Christ in the depths of his soul, who attempted to honor faith and reason, and who anticipated the response to the pope's call to open wide the doors of the church to the domains of culture, civilization, and progress. Not long afterwards, however, the Holy See clarified that recent statements by members of the church made on the occasion of the anniversary of Teilhard's death, should not be interpreted as any change in the church's previous judgment of the man and his work. This statement came four months before the then Cardinal Joseph Ratzinger, the future Benedict XVI, took over as prefect of the Congregation for the Doctrine of the Faith.

Thus, even now, the 1962 *monitum* on Teilhard de Chardin remains the official position of the magisterium on his work.

Unlike the other theologians described in this book, Teilhard has not in any way been rehabilitated by the magisterium either formally or informally, either during his lifetime or afterwards. The present pope's attitude toward Teilhard runs from a complaint that the *Constitution on the Church in the Modern World* exhibited too much of a French and Teilhardian influence to remarks in July 2009 when the pope said that Paul's vision of the world is "the great vision that Teilhard de Chardin also had: At the end we will have a true cosmic liturgy, where the cosmos becomes a living host."[34]

Nevertheless, in the scientific and theological communities, his work and influences are apparent. Perhaps, like another controversial scientist, Galileo, Teilhard will have to wait several hundred years for any official recognition or rehabilitation by the magisterium.

Chapter Two

YVES CONGAR:
APOSTLE OF PATIENCE

Introduction

Yves Congar, a French Dominican priest, was one of the pioneers in the church's theology of ecumenism and of a more prominent place for laity in the church. As do most pioneers who break new ground and explore new avenues, he encountered suspicion, hostility, active opposition, and sanctions from church authorities. For a time, he was banned from ecumenical work, including speaking and lecturing, and banished from France to Rome and then to England. Through it all, he managed to maintain a deep love for the church, and a loyalty to the Dominicans and to his own deeply felt insights. His scholarly work has had a profound impact on contemporary theology. Eventually, he was exonerated and became one of the most influential theologians at the Second Vatican Council. Shortly before his death, he was made a cardinal of the church.

The year 2004 marked the one-hundredth anniversary of the births of four theological giants of the twentieth century: Karl Rahner, Bernard Lonergan, John Courtney Murray, and Yves Congar. Besides sharing a common birth year, all four were theological pioneers whose impact on contemporary theological development is still felt today. As original and creative thinkers, all save Lonergan aroused suspicion and disciplinary action from Roman ecclesiastical authorities, but it was Congar who was most seriously and personally affected by his encounters with Vatican churchmen. In September 1956, Congar, in a letter to his mother, explained why he thought church authorities had silenced him: "What put me wrong (in their eyes) is not having said false things, but having said things they do not like to have said."[1]

Congar's deep concern for truth led him to continue saying things that some church authorities did not wish to hear, during a long and influential career that continued from late 1930s to 1982, when he published the last book of his nearly two thousand publications. For instance, one revolutionary claim he made was that the word *priest* in apostolic times referred to priests of the Jewish levitical order and that in the Christian dispensation, *priest* is correctly used only to refer to Christ and the baptized who share his priesthood— not to presbyters as ministers of the church hierarchy.

For most of his theological career, Congar worked under the intense scrutiny of Vatican authorities who dogged him with their continual accusations, suspicions, and restrictions on his writings and ministry. "From the beginning of 1947 to the end of 1956," he once wrote, "I knew nothing from that quarter [Rome] but an uninterrupted series of denunciations, warnings, restrictive or discriminatory measures, and mistrustful interventions."[2] The situation, however, was not destined to last forever, and his silencing was only a brief but painful interruption in a brilliant career of loyal service to the church. The church would eventually come to accept his views and honor him for them, but only after a long and difficult struggle with Roman authorities at the highest level. His personal and, until recently, unpublished, account of his dealings with what he called the "Roman hydra" are now available in *Journal d'un théologien 1946–1956.*

Congar once described himself as being a very impatient person: "I am impatient in little things. I am incapable of waiting for a bus."[3] But his long and tense relationship with ecclesiastical authorities, characterized by a limitless patience, proved otherwise. He believed that as a reformer he had to avoid the temptation to plant the seed, but then hurry it along and clear the field:

> Those who do not know how to suffer, do not know how to hope either. People who are in too much of a hurry, who wish to grasp the object of their desires immediately, are also incapable of it. The patient sower, who entrusts his seed to the earth and the sun, is also the man of hope….The cross is the condition of every holy work. God himself is at work in what seems to us a cross. Only by its means do our lives acquire a certain genuineness and depth.[4]

This wisdom, however, did not prevent him from being what he called a nuisance because of his continued prodding, exploring, challenging, and trying in whatever ways he could to bring about his vision of the church. His personal difficulties with church authorities contributed to both his work for ecclesial reform and his own spiritual growth.

Early Influences

Yves Congar was born in 1904 in Sedan, in the French Ardennes. At that time his compatriot, the Jesuit scientist Teilhard de Chardin, was teaching at a Jesuit scholasticate. Teilhard's writings on original sin and evolution would, like

Congar's on other topics, also eventually incur disciplinary actions from the Vatican. As a young man in his early twenties Congar spent three years in a Carmelite monastery, where he encountered Thomistic philosophy through the works of the renowned lay philosopher Jacques Maritain and the Dominican theologian Reginald Garrigou-Lagrange. Many years later, Lagrange, an influential consultant to the Holy Office, would become Teilhard's chief antagonist. Congar was also attracted to the Benedictines, having spent some time with them. In 1925, he decided to enter the novitiate of the French Dominicans at Amiens. Following his theological studies at the seminary at Le Saulchoir, near Paris in Étiolles, which had a strong emphasis on historical theology, Congar was ordained a priest in 1930. As early as 1929, he had recognized his call to labor in the cause of ecumenism. In October of 1931, he chose as the topic for his lectoral thesis *The Unity of the Church*.

Following his ordination, Congar taught theology for the next eight years at Le Saulchoir, which in the mid-1950s was a center of theological controversy, resulting in the dismissal of several prominent professors, including one of Congar's former professors, the Dominican theologian, Marie-Dominique Chenu. Nine years older than Congar, Chenu played a significant role in the latter's theological formation. Chenu introduced Congar to the work of the ecumenical Lansanne Faith and Order Conference, an ecumenical movement begun in Switzerland in 1927, and the thought of Johannan Adam Mohler, whose groundbreaking book on the church Congar would translate in 1938.

Other prominent scholars who influenced Congar's intellectual development during the period of theological revival in France were Étienne Gilson, Emmanuel Mournier, Pierre Maury, Jean Danielou, and the Russian mystic, Nicholas Berdyaev. He also studied Luther and Barth. Early in his academic career, Congar made contact with Karl Barth, the era's leading Protestant theologian, and in the spring of 1932, he befriended Dom Lambert Beauduin, an early pioneer in ecumenism who, at the request of Pope Pius XI in 1925, had founded a Benedictine monastery of biritual monks in Amay, Belgium. By the time Congar met him, Beauduin's critics had persuaded Rome to exile him to France because of suspicions aroused by his foundation and his ecumenical work with Anglicans and Eastern Christians.

Early on, Congar had become aware of the church's tendency to condemn innovations when Pius XI banned the reactionary Catholic movement L'Action Française in 1926, because it was primarily a lay movement. (It was later reinstated by Pius XII.) In his personal diaries, he wondered why the church always had to condemn, sometimes quickly and with no explanation. Congar was beginning to realize, in those early days, that church authorities more or less disowned anyone promoting the cause of Christian unity. He knew that the early pioneers "who had achieved anything and had opened up new avenues [were] bound to have difficulties."[5] Perhaps he was unconsciously preparing himself for all the problems and trials he would encounter in his own life's work for Christian unity and church reform.

Having met Abbé Courtier, a priest from Lyon and the originator of the idea of universal prayer for Christian unity, Congar was invited in 1936 to preach a series of sermons at the first Christian Unity Octave at Paris's historic Sacre Coeur church in the Montmartre section. These talks later formed the foundation for his book *Divided Christendom: A Catholic Study of the Problem of Reunion*, which easily passed the official censors and was published in 1937. This book, which first brought him to the attention of the Roman authorities, argued that other Christian denominations had at times preserved elements of Christianity better than the Catholic Church. Ten years later, he was still the object of criticism by the Roman curia for things he had said there, which the Vatican realized had people talking about ecumenism. The work of preaching for Christian unity became a focal point of Congar's own life and ministry. Every year thereafter, he was asked to preach in some part of the world each January during the annual celebration of the Christian Unity Octave.

Growing Tensions

In 1937, Congar received a first hint of concern from the Vatican, when the secretary of state, Eugenio Cardinal Pacelli, forbade him from being an official observer at an ecumenical conference that Congar himself had helped organize in Oxford, England. However, at least he was permitted to attend the conference. Years later, he would return to England, but under very different and rather unpleasant circumstances.

In 1939, Chenu and Congar were both called to Paris by the master general of the Dominican order and warned that serious difficulties had arisen from their theological writings. Congar's book *Divided Christendom* had raised concerns at the Holy Office, though it was not made clear to him precisely what the problem was. In that same year, Congar was drafted as a military chaplain. He spent 1940–45 as a prisoner of the Germans in Prussia, Saxony, and Silesia.

In March 1942, during his incarceration in Colditz, a high-ranking Vatican official publicly criticized him in the pages of *L'Osservatore Romano*, the official organ of the Holy See. Later that spring, bad news arrived in a letter from friends. He learned that his Dominican colleague Chenu had been dismissed as rector of the seminary at Le Saulchoir, and that a book Chenu had written, whose theological vision and method Congar shared, had been put on the church's Index of Forbidden Books. Congar felt that he himself remained unscathed only because he was outside the country.

In 1946, after the war ended, rumors began circulating about an impending crackdown from Rome, signaling a change in the direction of the church by Pope Pius XII. Concern in Rome about Congar's *Divided Christendom* still lingered and new objections arose to some of his other publications. In December 1947, he was refused permission to write an article on Catholic ecumenism requested by the World Council of Churches in preparation for a meeting in Amsterdam the following year. Meanwhile his highly popular book, *Divided Christendom*, was out of print but still very much in demand. His publishers asked him to prepare a new edition. His religious superiors required him to submit any revision for prior censorship to prevent further problems with Rome. The revision took Congar six months to complete, and on October 2, 1948, the manuscript was taken to Rome. Nothing more was heard of it until August 17, 1950, when he was told that, in light of the pope's forthcoming encyclical (published in 1950 as *Humani Generis*), certain additional changes were demanded, although he was not told precisely what they were. Congar later stated that this tactic of his superiors was actually their attempt to limit the role of Roman censors by allowing Congar himself to propose a satisfactory text. As so much had changed in the world of ecumenism since the work's first publication, Congar abandoned the project entirely. Reflecting on these events in 1966, he said that even though he would have had no problems from Rome in publishing a new edition, he felt that the ecumenical situation had changed too much: "That for which I was once reproached has now been accepted by all ecumenists."[6]

Ecumenical Activities

In 1947, a year before the Amsterdam ecumenical meeting of churches (which saw the formation of the World Council of Churches), Congar was asked by the organizers to submit a list of ten suitable persons to represent the Catholic Church. This request, no doubt, was due to his widespread reputation in the field of ecumenism. Congar meanwhile, had approached Cardinal Emanuel Suhard of Paris for advice and was authorized by him to write to the archbishop of Utrecht recommending ten or twelve official Catholic observers. Suhard was under the impression that Congar had received permission from Rome to name four observers, which was certainly not the case. The assistant secretary general of the World Council of Churches simply wanted to deal directly with Catholics who were well informed and sympathetic to the ecumenical movement. (Congar had a well-deserved reputation for openness among Protestants.)

Rome was eventually informed of these negotiations and on June 6, 1948, issued a *monitum* (warning), reserving to itself the right to appoint observers to the Amsterdam meeting. This gave Congar reason to hope that at least there would be some Catholic presence at the ecumenical gathering. His hopes were dashed, however, when on June 28 the cardinal of Utrecht informed Congar that the Holy Office would not grant authorization for any Catholic participation in the Amsterdam meeting. As it happened, Catholic experts were in the city during the meeting, but not as official observers and did not take part in any of the actual meetings. The whole experience taught Congar a painful lesson. It was also a major turning point in his life. He was, he said, not made for any kind of negotiations that demanded prudence, tact, and circumspection but he knew there was more to it than that: "I may have one of these gifts, but certainly not all of them. In addition, I was irremediably suspect and under surveillance; my actions, real or supposed, were interpreted in advance in a reprehensible sense."[7]

On December 20, 1949, apparently because of this incident, the Holy Office published guidelines for official Catholic participation in the developing ecumenical movement, which actually legalized, with careful restrictions, what was already being done in many places. Congar did not chafe at the restrictions, and he made it clear that he himself had never "either before or since, taken part in a meeting without the usual authorization, any more than I have ever published a line in contravention of the rule imposed upon me."[8] The rules and restrictions became even more stringent after the 1950 publication of *Humani Generis*, a condemnation of contemporary reforms of theology and of unapproved ecumenical undertakings, among other things. Ironically, the encyclical was published in the same year as Congar's groundbreaking and popular *True and False Reform in the Church*.

The ecumenical movement received another shock in 1950, when Pius XII defined as infallible the doctrine of the bodily assumption of Mary. Congar's strategy, he later recalled, was a renewed determination to be "as discreet as possible in overtly ecumenical matters, particularly as far as publications were concerned. I felt that the condemnation or formal disavowal of a book like *Cretiens desunis* would set the ecumenical movement back thirty years. At this particular juncture I could serve the cause best by keeping silent and by publishing nothing."[9]

In February 1952, the Holy Office barred a second edition of *True and False Reform in the Church*, including all translations. He was also ordered to submit all future writings, including even small reviews, directly to Rome for approval to publish. He readily complied but commented privately that such actions show the incredible narrowness of censorship. Despite this, some of his manuscripts were approved for publication.

On May 13, 1952, Congar joined other Catholic ecumenists to establish the Catholic Conference for Ecumenical Questions, with support from the Jesuit theologian and ecumenist, Augustine Bea. Pope John XXIII later appointed Bea to be the first cardinal president of the Vatican's Secretariat for Christian Unity and spearheaded the cause of ecumenism during the Second Vatican Council. Despite the church climate and Roman reservations about bringing ecumenical workers under one banner, Congar pushed ahead with the project, quoting the French spiritual writer, Père Lacordaire: "I have long thought that the most favorable moments for sowing and planting are times of trouble and storm."[10] The gathering took place in August 1952, with Congar providing theological treatises that were read at the meeting. He also drafted reports to be shared with the World Council of Churches, but since no official contact was allowed with this organization, his reports went unsigned.

While the ecumenical scene might have looked promising to Congar and other Catholic ecumenists, storm clouds were gathering. In the fall of 1953, the Vatican ended France's worker-priest experiment that had the full support of Emanuel Suhard, the cardinal archbishop of Paris. Pleas by French church officials to save the movement were ignored, provoking Congar to remark, "One can condemn a solution if it is false; one cannot condemn a problem."[11]

The Raid and Exile

The storm broke on February 6, 1954, when the master general of the Dominican order in Rome, the Spaniard Emanuel Suarez, appeared in Paris at the command of the Holy Office. Three Jesuit provincials from Paris, Lyon, and Toulouse were removed from office and four prominent and influential theologians (Boisselot, Feret, Chenu, and Congar) were banished from Paris. Thomas O'Meara provides a detailed and fascinating account of this in his "Raid on the Dominicans," *America*, February 5, 1994.

From his own previous altercations with the Holy Office, Congar was well aware of Rome's objections to his writings on ecumenism and church reform. If any theologians were to be disciplined, he would surely be among them. Congar was banned from teaching and ordered to obtain prior permission from Rome for any future writings. His response was immediate and blunt, calling the action absurd and simply inconceivable.

At his own suggestion, Congar was assigned to the Jerusalem's prestigious École Biblique where he wrote *Mystery of the Temple*, which had seven censors and took four years to publish. On February 9, he confided to his journal:

The bishops have bent over backwards in passiveness and servility: they have an honest and childlike reverence for Rome, even a childish and infantile reverence…for them this [Rome] is "the Church"….Rome is the Pope, the whole system of congregations which appear as if they are this church….The "Holy Office" in practice rules the church and makes everyone bow down to it through fear or through interventions. It is the supreme Gestapo, unyielding, whose decisions cannot be discussed.[12]

During his stay in Jerusalem, he was still ruminating about his experiences and wondered how far he should cooperate with the system:

> Today I am afraid that the absoluteness and simplicity of obedience is drawing me into a complicity with this abhorrent system of secret denunciations which is the essential condition of the "Holy Office"…if the Father General has taken sanctions against Chenu, Feret, Boisselot and me without reason—I mean without any other reason than the dissatisfaction of the "Holy Office" and its scribes of the papal court—he is working for the suspicions and lies which falsely burden us.…It is the system and the lies inherent in it which one must utterly reject.[13]

In September, Congar was called to Rome by the Holy Office for three months but was never actually interviewed. During his stay, he was not allowed to preach, lecture, or even meet with students in the parlor of his residence. In February 1955, he was assigned to Blackfriars, the Domincan house of studies at Oxford University, where he was under house arrest and still forbidden from any public talks, writings, or contact with Protestants. Later he recalled his time in England as a very hard eleven months of language difficulties, odious restrictions on his ministry, his movements, and his contacts with Protestants. In September 1956, he confides to his journal:

> Here I have endured unfathomable feelings of emptiness and absence. No one. Nothing. Certainly the weather is also to blame…caught in the rain outside and waiting under a tree for it to clear up, I begin to

weep bitterly. Will I always be a pauvre type? All alone, will I endlessly be carrying suitcases around everywhere? Will I always be without anyone and anything like an orphan....I weep for such a long time, perhaps an hour, and then again repeatedly...in view of the evidence that has now forced itself home on me that I have wasted my life and do not know to what curse I am exposed. [14]

Rehabilitation

Finally, in December 1955, Congar was assigned to the Dominican house in Strasbourg where the community, as a way of showing their respect and support in the face of Rome's disciplinary action, promptly elected him as prior. At that time, the Roman authorities had no direct supervision over the election of religious superiors. In this position he certainly had more personal freedom in preaching and lecturing, and communal support, but the cloud of suspicion still hung over him for his four years there. Eventually, with the help of Archbishop Weber of Strasbourg, he returned to Paris where he was able to resume his pastoral ministry and theological work.

With the advent of Pope John XXIII in 1958, the climate in the church began to change drastically. As a teacher of church history at the diocesan seminary, Roncalli had been denounced anonymously by a priest of the diocese of Bergamo because of his sympathy for certain authors who were persona non grata to the Roman curia. Legend has it that one of the first things the newly elected pope did was to go directly to the Holy Office, take his file, and write on it in large script, "I am not a heretic." Congar's personal influence on the Second Vatican Council (1962–1965) was far-reaching—from lecturing international groups of bishops to helping draft conciliar documents. In July 1960, he was appointed as a theological consultant to preparatory commissions, national hierarchies, and individual bishops, and was later made an official council *peritus*, a theological expert appointed to advise at a church council. He thought some of the texts prepared by the curia were better suited to the First Vatican Council and sent his own sixteen-page criticism. When the bishops of the world assembled, they decided to reject the drafts prepared by curial offices that listed and condemned numerous "errors" and "isms" of the modern world and that reminded many of the Syllabus of Errors published by Pope Pius IX in 1864.

Following the council, Congar was appointed a member of the Lutheran-Catholic dialogue and of the Pontifical International Theological Commission. He was at first somewhat critical of John XXIII because Congar thought that while the popular pope used sympathetic words and gestures, some of his decisions and church government contradicted the hope they embodied. These decisions, however, like the order for seminaries to return to teaching theology in Latin, may have been the work of a group of well-organized and influential curia officials. This entrenched group was active in opposing any kind of substantial reforms and was attempting to control the council by blocking any new ideas from the bishops. The bishops were so used to uncritically accepting decisions from Rome that they could not even see the contradiction when Rome condemned something the bishops had judged correct. However, after the death of John XXIII, Congar's evaluation of the pope's life and work were much more positive and enthusiastic.

Congar's hand can be discerned in almost every major document produced by the council fathers. Among major documents that bear his stamp are those on divine revelation, the church, ecumenism, missionary activity, priestly life and ministry, and religious freedom. Vatican II vindicated Congar and many of the theologians, including his friend Chenu, who had been silenced or disciplined by Rome. The truths to which they witnessed in their theological explorations and reflections gradually became assimilated into mainstream church teaching.

In 1966 Congar, along with Karl Rahner, Edward Schillebeeckx, and John Courtney Murray, was invited by Pope Paul VI to a special congress in Rome celebrating the theology of the Second Vatican Council. Again, in 1985, he was invited to a special synod of bishops to evaluate the impact of Vatican II, but Congar was eighty-one and living in a nursing home. In 1994, Pope John Paul II made Congar a cardinal, though, for reasons of health, he did not attend the consistory. He died shortly thereafter.

The road to such high ecclesiastical honors, which he never personally sought, was filled with much private pain and public humiliation. In the same moving letter to his mother mentioned earlier, he poured out his heart about the toll that the silencing took on him personally. He could be harsh at times in his observations, but usually right on target:

It is clear to me that Rome has never looked for and even now does not look for anything but the affirmation of its own authority. Everything else interests it only as a matter for the exercise of this authority. Except for a number of cases dealing with people of holiness and creativity, the whole history of Rome is about insisting on its own authority and the destruction of everything that cannot be reduced to submission. If Rome, 90 years late regarding the initiatives of the liturgical movement, now takes an interest in this movement, for example, it is so that the movement won't exist without it and won't be able to escape its control....Practically speaking, they have destroyed me as far as it was possible. Everything I believed and had worked on has been taken away...they have not, of course, hurt my body; nor have they touched my soul or forced me to do anything. But a person is not limited to his skin and his soul. When someone is a doctrinal apostle, he is his action, he is his friendships, he is his relationships, he is his social outreach; they have taken all that away from me. All that is now at a standstill, and in that way I have been profoundly wounded. They have reduced me to nothing and so they have for all practical purposes destroyed me. When, at certain times, I look back on everything I had hoped to be and to do, on what I had begun to do, I am overtaken by an immense heartsickness.[15]

Congar had a great appreciation for the virtue of patience and the role of the cross in the life of the would-be reformer that rings true even today: "Only when a man has suffered for his convictions does he attain in them a certain force, a certain quality of the undeniable and, at the same time, the right to be heard and respected."[16] In our own time, a similar sentiment was reflected in the words of Joseph Ratzinger, who, as Paul VI's cardinal prefect of the Congregation for the Doctrine of the Faith (the Holy Office in Congar's time), once said that suffering for the truth gives legitimacy to one's words.

Congar also appreciated the crucial role of history as it shapes the church and its teachings over the ages: "Acquiring knowledge of history is the surest way of acquiring confidence in the church. History teaches that nothing is new and that the church has survived sadder and more difficult situations. History is a school of wisdom and of limitless patience."[17]

Chapter Three

THE CENSURING OF
JOHN COURTNEY MURRAY

Introduction

One of the chief architects of the Second Vatican Council's *Declaration on Religious Freedom* was the American Jesuit priest John Courtney Murray. He had been speaking and writing extensively on church-state issues long before Pope John XXIII announced the Second Vatican Council, most notably to a less-than-enthusiastic gathering of cardinals at the Roman Basilica of St. Paul Outside the Walls on January 25, 1959.

Catholic doctrine on religious freedom had undergone very little development since the foundational teachings of Pope Leo XIII and Pius IX, who allowed for some tolerance of other religions by public authorities to prevent greater social evils. After World War II, there were calls for more cooperation among Christians in light of new world realities and problems. Added to this, from the Catholic perspective, was the emergence of the so-called "new theology," biblical and liturgical movements, especially in France, which generated new questions about freedom of religious expression and relations between religion and the state.

The military experience of American Catholics fostered close association with groups and individuals of other faiths and religious persuasions. This experience made Americans more willing to question restrictive Catholic teachings and attitudes towards Protestants and Jews. Prior to this time, any interfaith cooperation was seen as potentially diluting Catholic beliefs or compromising the traditional rigid attitude of exclusivity and moral superiority relative to other Christian denominations. The 1917 Code of Canon Law forbade Catholics from taking part in any non-Catholic liturgies.

In the first half of the twentieth century, there was no Catholic "ecumenical" movement, and the church wanted nothing to do with organizations like the World Parliament of Religions (1893) or even the World Council of Churches (WCC). As late as 1953, Catholic participation at the WCC's meeting in Evanston, Illinois, was forbidden. Gradually, however, lay Catholics began to recognize the value of cooperation among Christians, especially on common social and cultural projects. Even these early attempts were met with opposition from church authorities on the grounds that such joint efforts could lead to what they termed "religious indifferentism"—the belief that one religion is as true as another.

It was the issue of practical cooperation between Catholics and those of other faiths that first brought Murray to the attention of the Vatican, but it was during the 1940s that Murray began to develop and articulate a fully developed position on religious freedom proposing new—and to some, unacceptable—principles. The Vatican, through Murray's religious superiors, banned him for several years from writing or speaking on this topic. It was not until the Second Vatican Council (1962–1965) that Murray emerged as the most competent and influential theologian on religious freedom and one of the most highly respected *periti* in Rome.

Early Career

John Courtney Murray was born in New York City September 12, 1904, of a Scottish father (Michael John Murray) and Irish mother (surnamed Courtney). His baptismal name was Michael John; apparently the change was made sometime before he graduated from high school.

At the age of sixteen, he joined the New York Province of the Society of Jesus and by 1927, he had completed bachelors and masters degrees at Boston College. He then spent three years teaching at a Jesuit college in Manila. He returned to the United States in 1930 to begin theological studies at the Jesuit Woodstock College in Maryland, where he earned a licentiate in theology (STL) in 1934. He was ordained to the priesthood in 1933 and was sent to Rome in 1937, where he earned a doctorate in theology (STD) from the Jesuit-sponsored Gregorian University. He was then assigned to teach theology at Woodstock, a position he held until 1967.

As early as 1943, Murray had come under suspicion by some U.S. Catholic bishops, including Archbishops John T. McNicholas of Cincinnati and Samuel Stritch of Chicago, for his encouragement of ecumenical cooperation and his position on the development of doctrine. Murray first came to the attention of the Vatican also in 1943, when an auxiliary bishop of New York, Francis McIntyre, forwarded correspondence between him and Murray on interfaith and ecumenical interreligious cooperation, to Archbishop Amleto Cicognani, the apostolic delegate in Washington, DC. It is interesting to note that in 1943, Murray had helped draft and promote an interfaith statement, *Declaration on World Peace*, which might very well have been included in the material sent to Cicognani.

By 1945, Murray's expertise in these questions was beginning to be recognized. He was asked to prepare a memo on religious liberty for Archbishop Edward Mooney of Detroit, the chair of the administrative board of the National Catholic Welfare Council. In 1946, the Catholic Theological Society of America (CTSA) was founded, and Murray was elected to its Board of Directors. The CTSA's first president was a Redemptorist priest-theologian, Father Francis J. Connell, and the first secretary was Father Joseph Fenton. Both of these men would later become Murray's chief protagonists in a protracted and public debate on church-state relations. The CTSA Board asked Murray to start a series of publications dealing with the role of an authoritative church in a democratic society.

Two Catholic clerical publications played central roles in the evolving controversy on these issues. In 1940, the American Jesuits began publishing *Theological Studies* as a counterpart to several other prestigious Jesuit-sponsored European theological journals. The *American Ecclesiastical Review*, another such journal, had been established in 1889. These two publications became the voices of "progressive" and "traditional" theologians, respectively, on many church issues. But it was the question of religious freedom that fueled a heated and intense debate between the two in the 1940s and 1950s.

Beginnings of a Conflict

In 1941 Murray became the second editor of *Theological Studies* and, soon afterwards, the associate religion editor of *America*, another Jesuit publication. It was at this time that he also developed his interest in the issue of religion in a democracy, including freedom and the relationship between individual conscience and law. In 1946, Murray wrote his Jesuit provincial that he was moving away from an interest in "technical theology" to what he called "religion and society"—subjects such as "freedom of religion" (involving liberalism, church and state, etc.). From 1945 to 1948, along with his responsibilities as editor of *Theological Studies*, he had begun to read extensively in European sources on religious freedom. At one point, in 1947, he asked to be relieved of his editor positions at either *Theological Studies* or *America* in order to devote more time to this new area of investigation. Eventually he was allowed to relinquish *America* but was asked to stay on as editor of *Theological Studies*, which he did until 1964, contributing some twenty-one articles during that period.

At the second annual meeting of the CTSA in Boston of June 1947, Murray was to present a paper on the theology of church and state. He was unable to attend due to illness, and in his place Father Joseph Fenton of the Catholic University of America and colleague of Connell, was asked to deliver his own paper in Murray's absence. Although his approach was irenic, Fenton suggested that his paper would present views and attitudes distinct or divergent from Murray's, but it would "ultimately be advantageous to the Society to have heard two approaches to this particular section of the theological field."[1]

In 1948, Murray delivered his paper "Governmental Repression of Heresy" at the second annual meeting of the CTSA in Chicago. He suggested that classical Catholic "thesis-hypothesis" teaching on church and state, while appropriate for the secular European states, did not apply to the new situation in the United States.

The "thesis-hypothesis" taught that the "ideal" situation was for a Catholic state to recognize and favor the Catholic Church as the only true church. Catholicism should be the state religion in those places where Catholics were a majority and should uphold and embody Catholic beliefs and teaching in law. However, in places that did not have a Catholic majority, the state could recognize freedom of religion, at least until the "ideal" could be realized. This conditional recognition of freedom of religion was merely a concession, a lesser of two evils, the alternative being social discord.

A 1948 article in *La Civilta Cattolica* argued:

> In a state where the majority of people are Catholic, the Church will require that legal existence be denied to error and that if religious minorities actually exist, they shall have only a *de facto* existence, without opportunity to spread their beliefs. If, however, actual circumstances... make the complete application of this principle impossible, then the Church will require for herself all possible concessions....But in doing this the Church does not renounce her thesis...but merely adapts herself.[2]

Murray argued that other possibilities were tenable, such as the situation in the United States with its First Amendment guarantee that religious truths and values could be determined by the consciences of the citizens and not by the state. In responding to Murray's talk, Connell claimed that Murray was "out of harmony with the traditional belief and attitude of the Church for many centuries."[3] For Connell, the Catholic "confessional state" was the ideal and preferred arrangement where possible.

The Conflict Heats Up

Murray's views were beginning to gain acceptance among American Catholic intellectuals and theologians, but at the same time, his writings began to attract notice from Roman authorities. As early as August 1, 1950, Connell reported Murray to the Holy Office and the Congregation for Seminaries and Universities for the CTSA talk. Connell eventually sent more than twenty letters to Rome about Murray between 1950 and 1962, in an unrelenting campaign to have Rome publicly rein him in. At this same time, Pius XII published his encyclical, *Humani Generis*, which railed against new doctrines and novel ideas, including evolution and a tendency to minimize differences among churches. Although no names were mentioned, some commentators have suggested that Teilhard de Chardin and John Courtney Murray were among the targets of the papal document.

In the fall of 1950, Murray was in Italy for a meeting of Catholic ecumenists and met Monsignor Giovanni Battista Montini (later Pope Paul VI) *sustituo* secretary of state under Pius XII. Murray said that he found Montini "personally sympathetic with my 'orientations.' "[4] Montini asked Murray to prepare a memorandum on "The Crisis in Church-State Relationships in the USA."

In 1951, Murray published his first major article on church-state relations in the *American Ecclesiastical Review*, whose editor was Joseph Fenton of the Catholic University of America. In June of that year, Fenton summarized two opposing tendencies in the *American Ecclesiastical Review*. One was Murray's and the other was that of Father George Shea, a professor of dogmatic theology at Immaculate Conception Seminary, Darlington, New Jersey, and a strong ally of Connell and Fenton during the controversy with Murray.

In August 1951, Murray began corresponding with Fenton, writing some ten letters through June 1953. The initial exchange, according to Donald Pelotte, was "angry and tense." Murray asked to publish a response to Connell in the *American Ecclesiastical Review* without any comments by Fenton. Fenton, in turn, criticized Murray for publishing part two of a response to an *American Ecclesiastical Review* article in his own publication, *Theological Studies*, rather than in the *American Ecclesiastical Review*. The battle was joined. Murray spent the academic year 1951–1952 at Yale University as visiting professor of philosophy. On his return to Woodstock, he began working on several important articles on church-state relations from statements of Pope Leo XIII that were eventually published in *Theological Studies*.

Meanwhile, on April 24, 1951, Murray wrote to his Jesuit superiors in Rome inquiring about the memorandum he had written for Montini. At this point, all Murray knew was that it had been "called to the attention of the Holy Father...and had been committed to the hands of 'experts. Heaven help it, and me.' "[5] What Murray did not know was that in May 1951, Montini had sent Murray's document to several American churchmen, including Chicago's Cardinal Samuel Stritch, for their evaluation. Stritch delayed his response for a year and then told Montini that the report was not comprehensive and that he disagreed with Murray's contention that Leo XIII's teaching did not apply to the United States.

Also unknown to Murray was that the memorandum had been sent to Connell as well who responded with a five-page set of "Observations" arguing that Murray's adaptation "could not be harmonized with revealed truth."[6]

Connell continued to be supported in the controversy by George Shea and Joseph Fenton. In the meantime Murray received some support from a Jesuit colleague, Gustave Weigel, who, in a 1952 article in the Dominican philosophical journal, *Thought*, compared Connell's "static" with Murray's "dynamic" exposition of church-state relations.

Fenton accused Murray of making him a whipping boy in the theological battle and characterized the Weigel article as irresponsibly vicious and mendacious. On February 23, 1952, Connell again asked Rome to intervene this time by sending the apostolic delegate, Amleto Cicognani, a copy of a newspaper article favorable to Murray's position, apparently to provoke him into action. Cicognani took the bait: "I wish to assure you that I have recently had occasion to send to the Holy See certain material on this question. I am sure that it will be seriously considered but we know that the investigation and study take time."[7]

The Ottaviani Connection

In January 1953, Pius XII named Alfredo Ottaviani a cardinal and appointed him pro-secretary of the Holy Office. In March 1953, Murray published his first in a series of articles on Leo XIII in *Theological Studies*. In March, Ottaviani delivered a speech in Rome titled "Church and State" dealing with the church-state problem in light of the teaching of Pope Pius XII. Ottaviani reiterated the classical position on the state's duty to recognize the Catholic Church as the one true religion. In reply to those who accused the church of using a double standard, Ottaviani stated, "So be it. I do maintain precisely that there are two weights and measures to be used, one for truth and the other for error." [8] Referring directly to the situation in the United States, Ottaviani spoke of "two authors of opposing tendencies [without naming Murray and Shea] who published their writings in the *American Ecclesiastical Review*."[9] He then summarized, in English, the "mistaken theories" of those in the United States who held to "the liberalizing thesis." The source of Ottaviani's criticisms of Murray, as it turned out later, came not directly from Murray's own writings, but from a summary of the controversy written by Fenton that prompted Murray to accuse Fenton of misrepresentation. In the United States, the National Catholic News Service did not publish the full text of Ottaviani's criticisms, but rather a summary that had originally been published in *L'Osservatore Romano*. However, there was no doubt in anyone's mind that Murray was now firmly on the Vatican's radar.

In April 1953, Murray was hospitalized for heart problems in Baltimore and during his period of recuperation, the chill between him and Fenton began to thaw. Murray was distressed by the ongoing disagreement and suggested it would be possible to clear up any misunderstandings they might have had. He acknowledged that at times he had written "in a somewhat abrupt and at times perhaps careless fashion."[10] Murray suggested a meeting saying he had no intention of being personal in his criticisms and offered apologies if one of his early sharp letters responding to Fenton had been hurtful. Fenton replied that he was also "terribly nettled" and distressed because of the "bitter personal attacks" against him in *America* and *Thought*. He observed, "I have a horror of printed controversies between priests when these controversies tend to be personal."[11]

On June 12, 1953, Murray wrote to Robert Leiber, SJ, Pius XII's personal secretary, and the ghostwriter for many papal statements about the Ottaviani talk. In his reply, Leiber told Murray that Ottaviani's view "...only represents the private views of the Cardinal. It has no official or semi-official character. Your Reverence would do well, in my humble opinion, at least in a personal letter to the Cardinal, to correct what he erroneously characterizes as your opinion."[12] Murray immediately began to circulate this opinion of his superior in Rome in his own defense.

In a July 1953 letter to the noted American Catholic historian, John Tracy Ellis, Murray said that the Ottaviani talk might precipitate something in Rome: "I have it on the highest authority that our Holy Father was not pleased by the discourse and did not consider that it represented the true and full mind of the Church."[13] Murray made his position public in a July 23 *New York Times* article:

> Cardinal Ottaviani was speaking only in his purely personal capacity. His statement was neither an official nor a semi-official utterance. It was just the statement of a private theologian...speaking on his own authority. It is still entirely possible and legitimate for Catholics to doubt or dispute whether Cardinal Ottaviani's discourse represents the full, adequate and balanced doctrine of the church.[14]

A Vatican spokesperson seemed to uphold Murray's interpretation and added that the Ottaviani talk was unexceptional. Connell sent a copy to Ottaviani on the day the article appeared and, a few months later, a copy of an article about Murray. Connell warned Ottaviani that Murray would continue to hold this view contrary to church teaching until he was officially condemned.

In the summer of 1953, the rector of Woodstock, Joseph F. Murphy, SJ, had written to the Jesuit superior general, Jean-Baptiste Janssens, informing him of Murray's illness which he attributed in part to what he called the "unfortunate Roman statement [Ottaviani's]" of last March. In his reply to Murphy, Janssens said that Murray was not about to be censured, but that he should proceed cautiously and very thoughtfully and listen to the advice of experts. Murray was undoubtedly bolstered by the support of his religious superiors, academic colleagues, and soon even cardinals. On November 16, Murray dined with Cardinals Edward Mooney of Detroit and Samuel Stritch of Chicago, who were in Washington for the annual bishops' meeting. Mooney asked

Murray to "do a job" on Stritch who was cautious about Murray. Stritch told Murray that as a member of the magisterium he [Stritch] had to be cautious, but "he was glad that someone was attempting to cope...with these points which are a genuine source of difficulty to American Catholics."[15] Stritch allowed that *sensus fidelium* in the United States was definitely against the canonical thesis because it denies religious freedom. Mooney cautioned, however, "None of us today could go as far as Gibbons went."[16] Murray must have been sorely tempted to ask why not.

In November 1953, Murray's provincial, John J. McMahon, SJ, received a letter from Vincent McCormick, SJ, and the American assistant to Janssens in Rome, which Murray characterized as cryptic, enigmatic, and mysterious. Part of it was a mandate, which McMahon quoted to Murray on November 21: "I think the time has come for Fr. Murray to put down in simple, clear statements his full, present position regarding this Church-State question and send it to me for Fr. General. *sic mandatum.*"[17] On November 23, Murray requested time to respond to the order because it would be a major task to formulate the statement. It would help to know, he added, whether he was speaking "into a Roman climate of hostility or receptivity...am I *suspectus de haeresi* or simply the object of interest?"[18]

McCormick assured Murray on November 27 that he would be warned of any direct threat. The mandate for a clear statement came from Janssens's desire for Murray's view but "Rome has not expressed any fear for the orthodoxy of Fr. Murray, though not everybody in Rome, I presume, accepts his writing."[19] McCormick advised Murray to continue his work without fear because worry cripples the kind of work that he had undertaken.

Despite this assurance from his Jesuit superiors, and his meetings with the two cardinals in Washington, Murray was not overly optimistic about the courage of the American bishops. He wrote to Ellis in early July, "…we no longer seem to have any American Catholic bishops like Carroll, England, Hughes, Ireland.…Now they are all Roman Catholics."[20] Ellis concurred: "Something fine and bracing has gone out of the American Church and it is difficult to see how it can ever be regained."[21] Writing to Ellis again in December, Murray acknowledged his own disappointment with the average American bishop who "is so harassed by problems of administration that he has neither time nor inclination to tackle problems of high thought."[22] And, asking not to be quoted, "Sometimes I almost wish that Gallicanism had somewhat passed over this country…the French hierarchy are always disposed to close ranks and to defend the things French.… Moreover, they will be prepared to defend the freedom of the theological fraternity.…I cannot help but wish that a similar disposition was present here in this country."[23]

The Crisis Deepens

On December 6, 1953, Pius XII gave a talk to a group of jurists entitled *Ci Riesce*, in which he spoke about issues of freedom in the wider context of an international community and stated that his authority in these questions was final. Murray was again buoyed by the belief that the papal talk was in reality a clear response to Ottaviani and had actually disavowed the latter's position.

On March 25, 1954, Murray gave a lecture at the Catholic University of America on the pope's talk, *Ci Riesce*. Fenton interpreted the papal statement as supporting the traditional Catholic position that error has no rights. Most of Murray's lecture recapitulated the papal document, but Murray included what he thought was some advancement in the papal allocution that went beyond traditional Catholic teachings. He also reiterated Leiber's assurances that the Ottaviani talk was only a personal opinion and the papal address was a "public correction of impressions left by C. Ottaviani's construction of Catholic doctrine."[24] He noted that the Ottaviani speech had provoked public protests in diplomatic circles and that only the pope was competent to speak as the ultimate authority on questions of international life.

Reactions to Murray's talk from his opponents were predictable. Fenton termed Murray's claims that the Ottaviani talk was only his own personal opinion "utterly baseless." On March 27, Connell and Fenton contacted Ottaviani. This time, Connell pushed harder for a condemnation: "I am certain that Father Murray will continue to teach his views as long as there is no *explicit* condemnation by the Holy See, mentioning him or his writings *by name* [emphasis in original]."[25] Ottaviani assured Murray's critics that, although the question did not affect him personally, he believed it was his duty to act for "the common good, for the protection of the truth and for the defense of Catholic thought. Also patience and charity have limits in the light of justice and truth."[26]

On April 1, Ottaviani wrote to Cardinal Francis Spellman inquiring about Murray, and stated that Murray had said things that were untrue and personally offensive to Ottaviani. Spellman responded cautiously, asking for more details of what Murray had actually said that offended Ottaviani. Spellman also met with Ottaviani when he traveled to Rome, but nothing further came of Ottaviani's intervention and Spellman took no action against Murray. On his part, Murray took the advice of his superior and wrote an apology to Ottaviani that, claimed Murray, Ottaviani did not accept, although no documentation for this exchange is available other than Murray's reference to it.

In his March letter to Ottaviani about Murray's Catholic University talk, Fenton had also informed the cardinal that the University of Notre Dame Press had recently published a book titled *The Catholic Church in World Affairs* that contained an article by Murray on church-state relations. Ottaviani immediately went into action, pressuring the Congregation of the Holy Cross, which sponsors Notre Dame, to withdraw publication, although eventually this was revised to a demand for prior consultation before any second printing of the book. Ottaviani also brought pressure on the Congregation of the Holy Cross by directing a Holy Cross priest working for one of the Roman congregations to warn his religious order. The priest indicated that, after showing much patience and forbearance, the Holy Office was about to take "drastic measures and stringent rulings" against Murray, whose recent speech, "with disrespectful insinuations and untrue innuendos, indicates that benevolent counsels and gracious warnings have proved ineffectual."[27] The priest also conveyed Ottaviani's request to Father Theodore Hesburgh, president of Notre Dame, and other Holy Cross officials, for assurance that Murray would never be invited or permitted to preach, speak, or write articles for any Holy Cross institution.

The Silencing

The forces allied against Murray were already at work to settle the issue once and for all. In May 1954, Fenton was in Rome and was commissioned by Ottaviani to prepare two reports on Murray. The first had to do with Murray's chapter in the Notre Dame Press book: "Regretfully and after prayerful consideration, I consider it my duty to recommend that Z [Roman code name for Murray] be condemned *nominatim* by the Catholic public."[28] The second informed Ottaviani that some prominent U.S. bishops sided with Murray against Ottaviani, so Fenton recommended the appointment of bishops who sided with Ottaviani. Fenton was growing impatient but was assured by a friend in the Holy Office that action would be taken in the Murray case. It was not long in coming.

In a July 26, 1954, letter from Cardinal Giuseppe Pizzardo, secretary of the Holy Office, to Father Christopher O'Toole, the Holy Cross superior general, was informed that on July 7 the Holy Office had concluded that Murray must correct errors contained in his chapter in the Notre Dame Press book. Apparently a similar letter was sent to the Jesuit authorities, but unfortunately this documentation is not extant or, at least, not presently available from the Jesuit archives in Rome. This might also have been when the Jesuits placed Murray under prior censorship for his writings, though it may have occurred earlier.

On July 18, Murray submitted two articles to the Jesuit censors in Rome, one of which was his third article in a series he was writing on Leo XIII. He was informed they could not be published. He was also told that he should not provoke the Holy Office because it was on the edge about Murray. One of the Jesuit censors also indicated that Murray had enemies not only in the United States but elsewhere. He was advised to give up writing on the controversial question for the present.

Murray understood this warning as a way of gently being told that his work was over, which, for him, represented a defeat and failure of the first order. McCormick responded that Murray's work was far from over, but he ought to let the state-church question "...rest for the present...but I suppose you may write poetry. Between harmless poetry and Church-State problems, what fields are taboo I don't know...we'll try to keep out of controversy for the present."[29] Murray, somewhat depressed by the outcome, said he had returned all his books on the question to the library and would concentrate on other issues. According to some, Murray was silenced on orders from the Holy Office, but there is no official documentation to support this view. More likely, the orders to cease writing and speaking on the topic came from the Jesuit general in Rome, though probably at the instruction or suggestion of one of the Roman congregations—the usual procedure in the disciplining of a member of a religious order.

The Propositions

In a major article published in 1999 in *The Catholic Historian*, which included new research, Joseph Komonchak isolated four of the Murray propositions that the Holy Office had identified as worthy of censure. There appears to be some confusion about the precise number. In September 1954, Murray had written to Clare Boothe Luce that he had heard that out of approximately fifty propositions, twenty were condemned. However, he added that these rumors were false and calumnious.

It appears that Murray himself received the condemned propositions from the Holy Office. In comparing them later with an article published by Fenton in *American Ecclesiastical Review*, and noticing striking similarities, Murray concluded that Fenton was probably the author of the list of censured propositions. Fenton had received the censured propositions from the apostolic delegate on October 28, 1954. Fenton and Connell were told that Murray must retract the propositions in writing, and that Fenton and Connell were to monitor this, without indicating that the order had come from a higher authority. Although none of the censured propositions appeared in the Notre Dame Press book, Komonchak says, "This may suggest that the action against Murray had been well underway before his speech at Catholic University and that this essay gave the Holy Office a pretext for action."[30] As is often the case with many contemporary theologians charged with "ambiguity" by the Vatican, Murray denied that any of the condemned propositions were either ambiguous or necessarily held by him.

In March 1955, Murray spoke of going to Rome presumably to defend himself to the Holy Office, but McCormick threw cold water on the suggestion: "Some will say you have been summoned....I see no good to be gained by contacting his Em. O. He has been too badly hurt by this whole affair by what happened there and here."[31] For the next few years, Murray avoided controversy and began writing on other topics without abandoning his keen interest in the issue of religious freedom. Like Teilhard and Congar before him and Merton after him, Murray sought to circulate his views through other channels. Murray sent galleys of an article that he had been refused permission to publish to a Father Murphy in March 1957, with the advice to "use any of the substance of the article for any purpose" while prohibiting any "direct quotations, much less any reference to this article which, as it were, does not exist."[32] For Murray this was a friendly gesture: "this is no way to carry on theological argument....However, that's the way it is. Even so, one is not forbidden to make friendly gestures. And this letter, and the MS, is in the nature of a friendly gesture."[33]

Conclusion

In 1958, Murray wrote to McCormick asking to submit an article to *La Civilta Cattolica* on the Catholic constitutional problem raised by the candidacy of John F. Kennedy for pres-

The Censuring of John Courtney Murray

ident of the United States. Recalling the censure he was under, Murray said that, as for the counsel of prudence to keep silent, "I have observed the counsel, under assent to its prudence. Only now I wonder whether the time has come for counsels of prudence to cede to the claims of truth."[34] McCormick's response was swift and frank, advising Murray to be patient until the time was ripe when a statement could be made:

> I am afraid you do not know the Rome of today....No, we must be patient, some people never forget....I really think that you must wait for that, not expose yourself by trying to hasten it. In the end what is correct in your stand will be justified. Meanwhile be content to stay on the sidelines...deepen and clarify your own position, and be ready with your solution approved when the opportune time comes. That is not coming in the present Roman atmosphere.[35]

Although the atmosphere was soon to change with the election of John XXIII in 1959, the Holy Office at this time was preparing an official condemnation of the ideas of Murray, Jacques Maritain, and other Catholic thinkers. Only the death of Pius XII prevented this from happening.

On October 8, 1958, Pope Pius XII died. Angelo Roncalli, John XXIII, was elected and the atmosphere began to change. The pope called for an ecumenical council on January 25, 1959. The opportune time had finally arrived after his years of silence. Murray, along with John L. McKenzie, Henri DeLubac, M.-D. Chenu, J. Danielou, and Hugo Rahner, was at first "dis-invited" to be on the planning commissions for the first session, whereas Fenton had been called to Rome as Ottaviani's theological expert. During the first session,

Murray advised Baltimore's Cardinal Lawrence Sheehan on drafts of council documents. In the spring of 1963, during a break in the council, it was evident that Murray was still persona non grata in some official quarters when he, along with Godfrey Diekmann, Gustave Weigel, and Hans Küng, was barred from speaking at the Catholic University of America at the urging of Egidio Vagnozzi, apostolic delegate to the United States (1958–1967). In that same year, Murray published the book most associated with his name, *We Hold These Truths: Catholic Reflections on the American Proposition*.

Finally, on April 4, 1963, at the insistence of Cardinal Francis Spellman, Murray received his official invitation to attend the second session of the council as a *peritus* and later served as the chair of the commission drafting the document on religious liberty. At a meeting of the Commission on Faith and Morals, Murray encountered both Ottaviani and Fenton. Ottaviani did not "recognize or distinguish the tall figure of Father Murray. When he spoke...Cardinal Ottaviani, one hears, leaned over to his neighbor, Cardinal Leger, to ask who was speaking. The Canadian Cardinal, perhaps to spare Father Murray any unwelcome publicity at this point, replied simply *'peritus quidam'* " ["one of the experts"].[36]

In January 1964, Murray spent several weeks in the hospital recuperating from a heart attack. Soon thereafter, his provincial heard that the apostolic delegate, Vagnozzi, was upset about an article on the council Murray had authored for *America* because *periti* "are forbidden to organize currents of opinion or ideas, to hold interviews, or to defend publicly their personal ideas about the council."[37] Murray, apparently feeling more confident than ever, responded: "What business is this of the Apostolic Delegate? He is in no sense an official of the Council. He has no jurisdiction whatever over the activities on the periti....The Apostolic Delegate has elected to be my personal enemy and he has made statements about me throughout the country which are libelous."[38] The delegate later told Murray he had written to the Jesuit superior at the direction of the Holy See.

Murray made a substantial contribution to the final version of the Declaration on Religious Freedom. He also played a major role in getting the document back on track after Paul VI, strongly lobbied by curial conservatives, derailed it by deciding (on what has been called "Black Thursday" and the "Day of Wrath") to postpone the discussion and vote on the document to the fourth session. Murray's influence in both areas is related in detail in Alberigo and Komonchak's magisterial *History of Vatican II* and, more popularly, in Xavier Rynne's, *Vatican Council II.*

Murray's years of silence ended quickly and dramatically with the advent of "Good Pope John" and Vatican II. Murray identified what his opponents feared was "the affirmation of progress in doctrine that an affirmation of religious freedom necessarily entails."[39] For Murray, the development of doctrine was *"the* issue under the issues" at Vatican II" [emphasis in original].[40] John Tracy Ellis reported hearing Murray say at a dinner that Cardinal Newman's idea of the development of doctrine might well become one of the key ideas of Vatican II. The often-heard claim today that the teaching of the church cannot change is invariably met with the name of John Courtney Murray and the change in church teaching on religious freedom in which he played such a major role. Although he was dealing with a long-established tradition of doctrine on church and state, he anticipated the conclusion of a young German theologian at Vatican II, Joseph Ratzinger: "Not everything that exists in the Church must for that reason be also a legitimate tradition; in other words, not every tradition that arises in the Church is a true celebration of the mystery of

Christ. There is a distorting, as well as a legitimate tradition...[and]...consequently tradition must not be considered
only affirmatively but also critically."[41]

As for freedom in the church, Murray also proved prophetic
when he said that from the Declaration on Religious Freedom
a "great argument will be set afoot—now on the theological
meaning of Christian freedom. The children of God, who
received this freedom as a gift from the Father...assert it within
the Church as well as within the world, always for the sake of
the world and the Church." [42] Yet he was no radical, assuring
Paul VI that the basis of religious liberty was the dignity of
every human person. Murray was not comfortable with the
phrase "freedom of conscience," although he helped prepare
a draft statement on the topic for an American bishop at the
council.

James Carroll claims that in hindsight "it seems obvious
that his [Murray's] asking how the Church should respect the
conscience of non-Catholics would lead to his asking how it
should respect the conscience of Catholics."[43]

The lifelong struggle took its toll on Murray. In the spring
of 1964, he suffered another heart attack and, in mid-
October, a collapsed lung. Nevertheless, he was back in
Rome on December 7 for the historic vote in favor of the
declaration of which he had been the chief architect. He
prayed, it has been reported, that God would let him live to
see the end of the council, win or lose, vindicated or not.
One of his happiest days was when he was invited, along
with a number of other previously suspect theologians, to
concelebrate Mass with Paul VI on November 18, 1964.

He returned to the United States and Woodstock at the
close of the council and devoted himself to other issues such
as freedom in the church, the development of doctrine, and
atheism. He wrote six articles on the Declaration on

Religious Freedom, although when it was suggested he write a history of it, he declined saying he was "frankly tired of the whole subject."[44] In the spring of 1966, he was appointed director of the John LaFarge Institute in New York City, which brought him into contact with the issues of racism and ecumenism. He was also involved in Lutheran-Catholic dialogue and a church commission on conscientious objection. He died on August 16, 1967, at the age of sixty-two, in a taxicab while on his way from his sister's house in Queens to his office at the Institute in Manhattan.

Chapter Four

THOMAS MERTON:
THE SILENCED MONK

Introduction

Thomas Merton spent 27 of his 53 years in a Trappist monastery in a rural area of southern Kentucky not far from Bardstown and Louisville. Strict silence for most of the day was still an integral part of monastic life when he entered the Abbey of Gethsemani on December 10, 1941. Following the renewal of religious life initiated by the Second Vatican Council (1962–1965), the rigorous observance of the rule of silence was modified in most of the church's contemplative orders. While some Trappist communities still retained sign language, verbal communication at certain times and places was both permitted and encouraged.

Merton never really chafed under the older and stricter silence and found creative ways to get around it when he felt it necessary. At the same time, he experienced a growing desire for more solitude and deeper silence that eventually led him to live as a hermit for several years at the end of his life. Yet even during his relatively few years in the hermitage on the monastery's grounds, he managed to maintain lively contact both through written correspondence and personal visits with a wide variety of individuals, including bishops and parish priests, renowned scholars, prominent literary figures, and church and world leaders. He also managed to leave the hermitage now and then to visit friends in Louisville for a few beers.

Merton had an obsessive need to communicate his thoughts and something of his inner life through books, journal articles, reviews, and correspondence. He had a great deal to say on almost any subject. "Oh my God, he will never write again," was the initial reaction of Naomi Burton Stone, his longtime friend and literary agent when she heard he had entered a Trappist monastery.[1] How wrong she was! Many of his devoted followers who praised and gobbled up his earlier spiritual and devotional books were not at all happy during the volatile decades of the sixties when his attention and writings turned to cultural and social issues like racism, war and peace, and even liturgical renewal.

Complaints about his activism for social justice and for taking unpopular stands on nuclear war came from both his reading public and church authorities. As a result, Merton was silenced on writing about war and peace just at the time when he felt the most urgent need to speak out. The ban precipitated one of the major crises in his life, but, as with the rule of silence, he observed what he judged to be the spirit of the ban while finding creative ways to circumvent its letter.

Merton and the Censors

The first thirty years of Merton's tumultuous life—from his birth in France on January 31, 1915, to his conversion, vocation, and early years in the monastery—have been movingly detailed in his bestselling, much-translated, and influential autobiography, *The Seven Storey Mountain*, published in 1948, a book that won him world acclaim. Later in life he would distance himself from the work because he though it somewhat artificial. No doubt, it was the one book through which most people first encountered him.

In the early years of his monastic life, Merton struggled with the tensions inherent in his two vocations as a contemplative monk and as a writer. The resolution came in part once he received permission and encouragement from the highest ecclesiastical authorities to write for the good of the church and the order. In the attempt to combine both vocations, however, he was faced for the first time in his life with the reality of censorship. At first, he was docile and learned to overcome his strong abhorrence of censorship, a position he had passionately embraced during his academic career both in England and at Columbia University. His early writings on spiritual issues and lives of saints met with little serious censoring. Even the cuts he was forced to make on his autobiography do not seem to have bothered him much— initially the Trappist censors rejected it entirely because of the numerous references to sex and drinking they judged would not edify Catholic readers. He was also instructed that his religious name, Father Louis, was not to appear on any of his books, articles, or poems, and he was not permitted to provide either old or recent photographs to accompany his published works.

His early works, such as *The Sign of Jonas, The Secular Journal*, and *The New Man*, were either initially rejected or held up by the censors while he was forced to make changes. In some cases, it was only after months and even years of rewriting, pleading, and negotiating that he was able to get permission to publish certain books or journal articles. As his vocation as a writer-monk matured, and his need to have his voice heard on social issues became more pressing, Merton's attitude toward censorship changed and his struggles with censors became more sensitive and challenging. He began to feel more and more irritated by unnecessary and narrow restrictions placed on what he could and could not say on controversial issues facing both the church and the world, issues in which he had become increasingly interested and vocal.

By spring 1961, Merton's reputation and image as a writer of devotional books and biographies was undergoing a significant alteration. He debated whether he should write an unambiguous statement of his position on nuclear war. He felt that, as a cloistered monk, there was no other way for him to work actively for peace. Writing was his most valuable and effective contribution, as he realized through responses from the many peace activists with whom he had come into contact and who were his personal friends. In August, Merton decided that he must commit himself: "I have considered the possibility of writing a kind of statement—'where I stand,' as a declaration of my position as a Christian, as a writer and as a Priest in the present war crisis. There seems to be little that I can do other than this. There is *no other activity* available to me" [emphasis in original].[2]

On October 29, 1961, he wrote, "Yesterday afternoon at the hermitage, surely a decisive clarity came. That I must definitely commit myself to opposition to, and non-cooperation with, nuclear war."[3] He was conscious of his influence as a writer within the Catholic Church and even beyond, but felt a real need to exercise an even broader influence on the growing movement for peace, especially among Catholics. Many of his devotees, however, thought differently and began to accuse him of becoming an activist for racial justice and nuclear disarmament. They saw such activism incompatible with the traditional goals and purposes of monastic life, especially in an order as strict as the Trappists. Commenting on an article he had written in October, "The Christian Duties and Perspectives on Peace," and which he had discussed with the novices, he remarked that he knew "it will certainly not please many people."[4]

In December, he wrote to a friend, W. H. Ferry at the Center for the Study of Democratic Institutions in Santa Barbara: "I am having a bit of censorship troubles. This makes me think that one way of getting some of my stuff around would be to let your people mimeograph it and include it with your material. Would you consider this in some cases? This would not require censorship."[5] Merton did not consider this a violation of the censorship rules by which he was bound. The order's 1956 statutes on censorship required that "brief articles destined for periodicals of limited circulation and influence" required only the permission of the abbot."[6] It was to be the beginning of many years of clandestine circulation of his works to a substantial underground readership, especially for works that were rejected by the censors. Merton was smart enough to know that the circulation of an offbeat essay could be more effective in reaching an interested and influential reading public than an article in an official publication.

Ferry and others, including James Laughlin, his publisher at New Directions, disagreed. Merton wrote to Laughlin denying their insinuation that he was engaging in some kind of monkey business. He denied the charge: "Not at all. We have some very strict censorship laws, and I have hitherto been very conscientious about keeping them."[7] Merton reasoned that circulation of a couple of hundred copies is not, technically at least, publication and would not be wrong unless expressly forbidden by his superiors.

From February to June 1962, however, despite difficulties with the censors, he managed to publish several articles on nuclear war in noted Catholic publications such as *Commonweal*, the *Catholic Worker, Jubilee, Blackfriars,* and the *Catholic Peace Fellowship*. During this period, he was also editing *Breakthrough to Peace*, comprised mostly of articles that had already been approved or published. Nevertheless, he still suspected—correctly as it later turned out—that it would be what he called a disaster were he to submit the whole manuscript to the censors. As an alternative, he suggested to Laughlin that New Directions publish the work without Merton's name on it. He would write a preface and submit it to the censors apart from the manuscript with the hope that it might be passed.

Opposition Increases

Merton anticipated public opposition to his increasingly vocal anti-war position: "It is clear to me that under cover of being honest, frank and just, I have been too eager to speak and too eager to say things that a few people wanted to hear—and most people did not want to hear."[8] In March, he wrote to a correspondent responding to a question, "Am I unpopular because of the writing on peace? You ask this. The answer is yes and no. Unpopular with some bishops, yes. Probably get hit over the head."[9]

One prominent complaint appeared in the March 16, 1962, issue of the *Catholic Standard*, the official organ of the Archdiocese of Washington, DC. A lengthy editorial challenged Merton's February article in the February 9, 1962, issue of *Commonweal* ("Nuclear War and Christian Responsibility") and charged him with "a startling disregard of authoritative Catholic utterances and unwarranted charges about the intention of our government toward disarmament."[10] Merton received the editorial from John Tracy Ellis, noted Catholic historian at the Catholic University of America. In his response to Ellis, Merton privately accused the editorial of misquoting him, dismissing him as an absolute pacifist, and wrong in implying that Merton claimed the pope had made a statement against all war. The paper's editor, Washington auxiliary bishop Philip Hannan, was a former Army chaplain and paratrooper whom many believed was the source of the editorial castigating Merton. (Hannan would later become one of the most vocal critics of "The Challenge of Peace: God's Promise And Our Response," a pastoral letter published by the U.S. Conference of Catholic Bishops on May 3, 1983.)

Merton's perceived dismissal of the relevance of the Catholic just-war tradition to the nuclear age that he once described as a boat that has "slipped its moorings and is now floating off in mid-ocean a thousand miles from the facts" provided some ground for the charge.[11] The accusation, however, was not completely accurate. Merton had already written an essay entitled "War in Origen and St. Augustine" specifically to pacify traditionalists and the censors by writing about war in the context of traditional Catholic moral teachings. In a letter to Gabriel Sortais, the abbot general in Rome, Merton said: "I am in no way a pacifist in the way he [a censor] condemns me....I only say that *total* war, *massive* nuclear destruction, without distinction between the combatants and the civilians, is against Catholic moral doctrine" [emphasis in original].[12]

Nevertheless, Merton's own pacifist view was evident especially in *The Cold War Letters*, (October 1961–October 1962), a collection of 111 letters that had been mimeographed at the abbey and widely circulated among his friends and correspondents. He had permission to write and distribute them because the abbot, Dom James Fox, interpreted the censorship laws as applying only to writings that could reach the general public. He apparently had no idea that restricting publication to what he thought was a private audience would result in the materials having such a widespread influence beyond that audience. In *The Cold War Letters*, Merton referred Catholics to papal principles on war, though he himself wanted a clear and strong condemnation of all nuclear war from Rome:

> One would certainly wish that the Catholic position on nuclear war was held as strict as the Catholic position on birth control. It seems a little strange that we are so wildly exercised about the "murder" (and the word is of course correct) of an unborn infant by abortion, or even the prevention of conception which is hardly murder, and yet accept without a qualm the extermination of millions of helpless and innocent adults, some of whom may be Christians and even our friends rather than our enemies. I submit that we ought to fulfill the one without omitting the other.[13]

The Ax Falls

Behind the scenes, there were developments within the order that would affect Merton directly. On January 20, 1962, Dom James Fox received several pieces of correspondence from the abbot general, Dom Gabriel Sortais. One letter was addressed to Merton; though Fox kept it, only giving it to Merton on April 26. This could have been, some have surmised, his own way of providing Merton with time to have more articles published before the ban on his writings:

> It seems finally that the opposition of censors and of the Abbot General (not to mention the Abbot General's sec-

retary) has become intransigent. Yesterday, Rev. Father gave me a bunch of letters and reports, the main item being a letter of the General dated Jan. 20th, which Reverend Father for some unaccountable reason had been saving up…the decision seems to be (it is not absolutely definite) that I am to stop all publication of anything on war. In other words I am to be in effect silenced on this subject for the main reason that it is not appropriate for a monk, and that it "falsifies the message of monasticism."[14]

Also with the letter was a request from one of the censors in Rome that Merton not send him any more materials for censorship. Merton explained to his peace activist friend Jim Forest, on April 29:

For a long time I have been anticipating trouble with the higher Superiors and now I have it. The orders are, no more writing about peace. This is transparently arbitrary and uncomprehending, but doubtless I have to make the best of it…the order is not yet absolutely beyond appeal and I can perhaps obtain some slight modification of it. But in substance I am being silenced on the subject of war and peace.[15]

The modification he spoke of was probably the possibility of publishing *Peace in the Post-Christian Era*, which he had prepared; but that was not to happen, at least for some time.

Merton responded dutifully to Sortais, "I want to accept wholeheartedly and with joy, the decision never to write anymore on war" and confided to his journal that it was a "relief to be finished with a struggle that few or none would appreciate."[16] He then explained to Sortais that he had a manuscript ready for publication and asked if it might be possible to send it to the censors. This was the manuscript of *Peace in a Post-Christian Era*, a collection of reworked articles that already passed the censors. It was a last-ditch attempt to get it published: "There are quite a lot of well informed people who think I am not altogether wrong. The article 'Peace... Responsibility' has appeared in *Commonweal* in early February. Shortly after, the Lenten Pastoral of the Cardinal Archbishop of Chicago was on peace. And this pastoral contained some ten sentences copied exactly from my article."[17]

A May 26, 1962, reply from Sortais was blunt. Sortais said he realized that Merton knew he was not the only one to talk about the problem of nuclear war and not the only one who inspired the archbishop of Chicago. He then distinguished between teaching that belongs to the hierarchy and those they delegate, and prayer that belongs to the monk. Merton's life as a monk would be more influential in the cause for peace than his writings and he asked him to renounce the publication of the prepared manuscript and to abstain from any more writing on nuclear war.

Merton concluded that for the time being, at least, the decision was permanent. The same order would be repeated twice again before the end of his life. Not until close to his death did the censors lift their ban on his writing on certain topics and require him to submit all writings to prior censorship.

By June, any such hopes of a modification of the silencing order had vanished:

I have written a whole book [*Peace in the Post-Christian Era*] but it has all been forbidden without even going to the censors. I have just been instructed to shut my trap and behave which I do since these are orders that must be obeyed and I have said what I had to say. I will send you a mimeographed copy of the book if I can. Meanwhile, with the letter of course you can use them discreetly, and I see no objection to their being quoted in class in a private school.[18]

At the same time, he began to find ways to circulate the manuscript. The stencils for the book were finished just as the silencing order arrived, and Merton saw no point in wasting them. He began to send mimeographed copies of the forbidden work to several of his correspondents, warning them to use the materials discreetly. Those friends included Jim Forest, Daniel Berrigan, Dorothy Day, and the publisher of *The Pax Bulletin*, a British peace periodical.

To another correspondent, Merton explained that his highest superiors had forbidden publication of *Peace in the Post-Christian Era* and none of it can or should be published as it stands:

However, I might make one slight exception. Actually, we are permitted to print material in "very small publications" without further permission. I think that if you just lifted a paragraph here and there without further identification, once in a while and just use it; there would be no real objection. However, when it comes to actually publishing significant parts of the book, I am afraid we are forced to set that aside for good or at least until there is some new decision from Rome.[19]

But there would be no new decision for a few years and certainly not from Sortais, whom Merton once described as "our patriotic French general, a staunch Gaullist and a most humorless chauvinist.[20]

Silence Speaks

In letters to friends following the silencing, Merton reacted at times with both caustic humor and scarcely concealed anger:

The Peace Book...is not to be published. Too controversial, doesn't give a nice image of monk. Monk concerned with peace. Doesn't give a nice image of monks. Monk concerned with peace. Bad image. Bad image. Monks in NY State have fallout shelters paid for with monks bread as advertised with pictures of sub human monks in NY Daily News: good image of monk, fine go ahead.[21]

He argued in a very sarcastic vein in an April 29 letter that he was trying to salvage the monastic reputation with his passionate protest against the arms race, not bring it into disrepute:

Imagine that: the thought that a monk might be deeply enough concerned with the issue of nuclear war to voice a protest against the arms race, is supposed to bring the monastic life into *disrepute*. Man, I would think that it might just possibly salvage a last thread of repute for an institution that many consider dead on its feet. That is really the most absurd aspect of the whole situation, that these people insist on digging their own grave and erecting over it the most monumental kind of tomb stone [emphasis in original].[22]

In a 1963 letter to the French philosopher, Jacques Maritain, he was still smarting at the abbot's view that a Trappist monk writing on peace falsifies the message of the contemplative life. It was, the abbot said "a hateful distraction, withdrawing the mind from the Baby Jesus in the Crib."[23] Merton could not resist a flippant comment to Maritain: "Strange to say, no one seems concerned at the fact that the crib is directly under the bomb."[24]

In a letter to Daniel Berrigan, Merton says his writings are called "dangerous, subversive, perilous, offensive to pious ears and confusing to good Catholics who are all at peace in the nice idea that we ought to wipe Russia off the face of the earth. Why get people all stirred up?"[25]

His peace-activist friend, Jim Forest, accused Merton of bending over backwards trying to please the censors and not really saying what he meant. Merton acknowledged in a July 6, 1962, letter to Forest: "I was bending in all directions to qualify every statement and balance everything off, so I stayed right in the middle and perfectly objective, and so on, and then at the same time tried to speak the truth as my conscience wanted it to be said. In the long run the result is about zero."[26] Laymen have leeway, he added, "After all, there is not much that the bishop can do to you guys."[27]

Between October 1961 and June 1962, despite his problems with Trappist censors over *Peace in a Post-Christian Era*, Merton managed to get significant parts of the work into print in other forms. In September 1962, New Directions published *Breakthrough to Peace* with an introduction by Merton titled "Peace: A Religious Responsibility." This essay was a touched-up version of something he had written for *Peace in a Post-Christian Era*. The preface would make it perfectly clear where he stood on the issue of nuclear war. In the summer of 1962, he was working with Thomas P. McDonnell on an anthology, *A Merton Reader*, eventually published in 1962 by Harcourt Brace, which included "Religion and the Bomb," retitled, perhaps as a way of vindicating himself, "May 1962"—the year of his silencing.

Merton's cautious attempt to navigate the minefield of controversy on questions of nuclear war stemmed from his desire to remain in the church and speak from the church: "...my position loses its meaning unless I continue to speak from the Center of the Church. Yet that is exactly the point: where is the true center? From the bosom of complacent approbation by Monsignors?"[28]

Along with the somewhat clandestine circulations of mimeographed manuscripts (Merton once commented that private circulation goes much further), he resorted in 1963 to writing under various pen names such as "Benedict Monk" and "Benedict Moore" for articles published in *The Catholic Worker*.

On October 11, 1962, the Second Vatican Council began and the following year Pope John XXIII published his encyclical *Pacem in Terris*. Merton lost no time indulging in a bit of gloating. He wrote to the abbot general at Easter what he termed a cheeky letter: "Fortunately [the Holy Father] does not need to be approved by the censors of the Order in America, for they said very energetically last year that this thesis, when I proposed it myself, was wrong, scandalous, and I don't know what more."[29]

This was certainly a tactical mistake because he was asking at the same time whether he could revise his unpublished book in light of the new encyclical. The response was prompt and harsh as he recounts to Leslie Dewart, a Canadian philosopher at St. Michael's College at the University of Toronto. Merton says he was refused categorically because, among other things, "I am incompetent and my opinions are of no value since I don't know what I am talking about in the first place....I do, however, still have a Christian conscience...and will have to do what I can short of publication on this precise subject"[30] This was the third rebuff from Dom Sortais.

Merton never missed an opportunity to send his writings to influential people like Maritain with the suggestion that if he knew anyone who might be interested, Maritain could pass the copy on to them. In May of 1963, he wrote to Ethel Kennedy explaining his banned book and sent her a copy for the files: "I wrote a book on peace which the Superiors decided I ought to bury about ten feet deep behind the monastery....I mimeographed it and am sending you a copy, just for the files or who knows maybe the President might have five minutes to spare looking at it. If you think he would, I will even send him a copy."[31] Likewise, he told Bishop John Wright, who was favorably impressed with the book and had circulated copies to some council *periti*, that he could send him more copies adding that "even though the book was not published, I am happy to think that the work was not wasted."[32] Merton was even in touch with another controversial author, Henry Miller, alluding to the fact that both of them had written "banned books."

On November 16, 1963, Dom Gabriel Sortais died. Merton had no illusions that a new superior would make a great deal of difference to his writing on war and peace. The new abbot general, Dom Ignace Gillet, took office early in 1964 and continued his predecessor's ban on Merton's writings, although he eventually allowed Merton to write about peace, but not about war. As late as March 1964, Merton wrote to Karl Rahner, "I am too often discouraged in encounters with the obtuseness of certain critics, and find myself in a position where I am forbidden to speak on one of the most urgent issues of our time: nuclear war. In this country where so many theologians are proposing complacent and totally un-Christian arguments in favor of the bomb, I am not permitted to speak out against it. I do ask you to pray for me and for us all."[33] He was concerned, among other things, as to how the ban would be seen by others, and that the church would be judged as unresponsive to new challenges of the modern world.

In July 1964, by which time the atmosphere in the church and in the order had begun to change, he was informed that his controversial and originally banned essay, "The Christian in World Crisis," could be published in a new work, *Seeds of Destruction*. In the essay, it was clear that he was totally opposed to Augustine's justification of wars of mercy. For him, the real heart of the forbidden book had finally seen the light of day:

> Now this would never have happened if Dom Gabriel had not been so stringent with the other three articles, which would have been used in *Seeds of Destruction* if he had not forbidden their reprinting. Thus in effect the very thing he wanted to prevent most has happened because of his own authoritarianism. This is something to think of when we think of religious obedience. The Church is not entirely run by officials.[34]

Merton and Religious Obedience

In contemporary church life, many theologians have been silenced or disciplined in some way during the past fifty years, including Teilhard de Chardin, Yves Congar, and John Courtney Murray. In most cases, this has been accomplished with little or no public notice, let alone organized opposition, unlike the more highly publicized Vatican actions against Charles Curran or Hans Küng. Yet the same question arises in each case—both from the individual silenced and from his supporters, especially when the disciplined individual is a member of a religious order with a vow of obedience: *Why obey?* Merton asked himself the same question: "Shouldn't I just blast the whole thing wide open, or walk out or tell them to jump in the lake?"[35]

As early as 1961, when the abbot general had instructed Merton not to write about Teilhard de Chardin's revolutionary book, *The Divine Milieu*, Merton acquiesced but groused in his personal journal: "I have no obligation to form my thought or my conscience along the rigid lines of Dom Gabriel. I will certainly accept and obey his decision, but I reserve the right to disagree with him."[36] When it came to the silencing order a year later, he revisited the issue of religious obedience: "One is faced with the very harrowing idea that in obeying one is really doing *wrong* and offending God."[37] And again, "There is also a culpable silence. Silence is not an absolute, not an end in itself."[38]

Merton was also deeply concerned about what he called complicity in observing the silencing, and at the same time what effect his disobeying the silence would have on others:

> ...silent complicity is presented as a greater good than honest, conscientious protest. This is supposed to be part of my vowed life and this is supposed to give glory to God. Certainly I refuse complicity. My silence itself is a protest and those who know me are aware of the fact. I have at least been able to write enough to make that clear. I have been able to write enough to define the meaning of my silence. Apparently, I cannot leave here in order to protest, since the meaning of any protest depends on my staying here, or does it? This is a great question.[39]

Merton was also deeply concerned about the consequences of not staying where he was and that there were always rumors flying around that he had left the hermitage, the order, or the church:

Why would I do this? For the sake of the witness for
peace? For the sake of witnessing to the truth of the
Church, in its reality as against this figment of the imag-
ination? Simply for the sake of blasting off and getting
rid of the tensions and frustrations in my own spirit,
and feeling honest about? In my own particular case,
every one of these would backfire and be fruitless. It
would be taken as a witness against the peace movement
and would confirm these people in all the depth of their
prejudices and self-complacency. It would reassure them
in every possible way that they are incontrovertibly right
and make it even more impossible for them ever to see
any kind of new light on the subject.[40]

For Merton, the ultimate solution to the crisis of obedience was love that, for him, was synonymous with obedience. He knew he was thought of as a disturbing element, as
were the prophets, and he was content with that judgment.
He was not deliberately seeking to disturb others, but only
to be true to his conscience. As for the restrictions with
which he had to deal faded, he described the inner faith
stance that helped him survive and continue writing:

I am where I am. I have freely chosen this state, and
have freely chosen to stay in it when the question of a
possible change arose....This means accepting such
limitations as may be placed on me by authority, and
not because I may or may not agree with the ostensible
reasons why the limitations are imposed but out of love
for God who is using these things to attain ends which
I myself cannot at the moment comprehend. He can
and will in his own good time take good care of the
ones who impose limitations unjustly or unwisely. That

is his affair, not mine....I find no contradiction between love and Obedience and as a matter of fact it is the only sure way of transcending the limits of arbitrariness of ill-advised commands.[41]

Near the end of his life, Merton spoke of conscience as involving a community of people:

...the Christian conscience is not just an individual conscience with Christian traffic laws, but it is a kind of collective conscience. Some people tend to over correct this idea and swing away from the individual notion towards a Communist view of things that there is just one conscience for everybody, the conscience of Christ; there is one mind for all Catholics, it is the mind of the Church, and the mind of the Church is something that is outside each individual and everybody gets lost in it...the real difficulty in defining a Christian conscience is that it is neither collective nor individual. It is personal and it is a communion of saints....In the old days they used to talk about "the mind of the Church," and that meant that you had to read the encyclicals and knew what the Pope had said and agreed with him. Now, of course the "mind of the Church" is that if you disagree with the Pope, you represent the mind of the Church! Neither is right....The real Christian conscience is way down in this depth where one feels at the same time a complete personal conviction...and at the same time I know that I am basically united with all that the saints and the Church have ever thought. You can have this and still disagree, which is the great thing. Because when Christians disagree, as they must, over accidental things, underlying it should always be this sense of security and unity in which they are united below their disagreement. This is something we really need today in the Church. Instead, people act and react purely as individuals and from individual standpoints rather than upon this basically Christian conscience which is universal and which permits individual differences.[42]

By summer 1967, Trappist rules about censorship had changed dramatically. Paul Bourne, who was considered more liberal, had been appointed one of the order's censors by Sortais. It was Bourne who finally informed Merton that he would no longer be required to submit his writings for censorship and that he would have no more trouble. Merton had been given the green light, yet he continued to send his writings to the censors right up to his bizarre death by electrocution in Bangkok in 1968, shortly after he had given a talk at an international conference on monastic spirituality to a gathering of seventy monks and nuns. He was anointed by Rembert Weakland who, ironically, was not a Merton fan because of Merton's disparagement of the Benedictines as inferior monks and hyper-activists. Weakland liked Merton's social justice writing but was critical of his more serious mystical works, which he thought too academic. Nor was Weakland impressed by Merton's talk at the conference, which he claims did not meet the aims of the meeting and disappointed the group. He acknowledges that he did not know Merton as a person very well: "He was always polite with me, but I could sense a bit of aloofness around superiors, not surprising given his troubled relationship with Abbot James Fox, his former superior at Gethsemani. At times his self-assurance bordered on arrogance."[43]

Long after his death, however, Merton was still a subject for a kind of posthumous censuring. In 2005, the United States

Catholic bishops undertook to write a catechism based on the Catechism of the Catholic Church but adapted for use in this country. The project was headed by the then-bishop of Pittsburgh, Donald W. Wuerl. Profiles of prominent Catholics, including Merton, were chosen to head each of the book's individual chapters. Two conservative Catholics, however, objected to including Merton because he was, in their judgment, a lapsed monk who had flirted with Buddhism during the latter years of his life. Consequently, Merton's biography was dropped from the project because, as Bishop Wuerl commented, "young people don't know who Merton is."[44]

EPILOGUE

The theologians—whose personal stories of conflicts with church authorities are recounted here—lived most of their lives and accomplished most of their theological work before the Second Vatican Council (1962–1965). In 1959, when the council was announced and initial preparations were begun, three of them were still writing on various church issues. Two of them participated personally in the council and had a direct influence on some of its major documents. All three lived through at least some of the developments in the post-conciliar period.

Their names and writings are familiar to students of theology and church history and to many Vatican II–era Catholics today. Probably few are aware of the intense sufferings that these individuals endured for their persistence in deep, personal commitments to the church and their religious orders. What sustained all four of them was their need to maintain their own integrity and personal responsibility to speak to the church what they believed were truths that needed to be spoken, even if the church was not always ready to hear them, much less embrace them.

Each suffered various forms of disciplinary actions from ecclesiastical authorities. They were banned from writing and publishing on certain topics and lost teaching positions. They faced ongoing suspicion and criticism of their theological contributions, were subjected to constant censorship, were refused permission to travel or participate in various professional meetings, and were barred from receiving academic honors from institutions. At times, they even endured temporary or permanent exile from their native countries.

Many readers will be surprised to learn of the lengths to which some ecclesiastical authorities were willing to go in order to maintain control over the theology of individuals whose writings were judged "ambiguous" or "confusing to the faithful." Others might defend such tactics as part of the church's responsibility to "protect the Deposit of Faith" by discerning what is compatible and what is "harmful to the Catholic community" who has the right to hear the truth.

In today's church, an increasing number of younger theologians are not members of the diocesan clergy or religious orders, but are single or married men and women, members of the laity, many of whom teach in seminaries and Catholic institutions of higher education. These theologians are less susceptible to disciplinary actions against them by the Vatican, although they are, at times, the objects of investigations and critical comments from the local bishop or bishops' conferences. Interestingly, however, neither the Vatican nor the U.S. bishops have been successful in removing Daniel Maguire, a resigned priest and divorced layman, from Marquette, a Catholic university in Milwaukee, Wisconsin. Maguire did, however, provoke the U.S. bishops in March 2007 to publicly warn Catholics about two of Maguire's published pamphlets on contraception and abortion and one on same-sex marriage.

At the insistence of the Vatican in 2001, the U.S. bishops drew up norms to implement John Paul II's apostolic constitution, *Ex Corde Ecclesiae*. The requirement of a *mandatum* from the local bishop for theologians teaching "sacred sciences" at Catholic institutions was seen by some not only as a way of reinforcing the Catholic identity of an institution, but also of exerting more control over lay theologians. Others view it simply as a way to ensure that Catholic theologians will not impart private opinions as the teaching of the church.

To date, there has not been a case of ecclesiastical authorities disciplining any Catholic lay theologian by the refusal or withdrawal of a *mandatum*. Church authorities still have the power, however, to deny a lay theologian a teaching position in a Catholic institution because of public positions judged to be in conflict with church teachings. This occurred in 2008 when Rosemary Radford Ruether was refused an endowed chair in theology at the University of San Diego because of her positions on abortion and the ordination of women.

None of the individuals considered in this work objected in principle to the responsibility of the magisterium to require theologians at times to defend, reexamine, clarify, or even reformulate certain assertions. While some might have chafed over censorship requirements, they all cooperated with such regulations in good faith. This does not mean, however, that they did not seek ways to circumvent censorship by the use of pen names and underground circulation of their writings among friends, supporters, and academic peers.

The partial biographies here might raise some interesting questions: has the relationship between theologians and the church today changed from the periods in which these theological giants flourished? What can we learn from the experiences that shaped their spirituality? Is their example of compliance one that is still possible and useful today? Could we have examined the lives and works of other individuals from post–Vatican II church life and theological endeavors in the past forty years?

Undoubtedly, the most famous case was that of the Swiss theologian Hans Küng, a former colleague of Joseph Ratzinger, who as head of the Congregation for the Doctrine of the Faith (CDF) surely played a crucial role in John Paul II's decision to revoke Küng's license to teach as a Catholic theologian. We now know that Küng himself also struggled with the issue of voluntary silence:

> I have long since also asked myself....Should I now keep silence on the question of infallibility for all time? Doubtless that would be extremely welcome to Rome and is probably what people in Rome expect after the 1973 declaration *Mysterium ecclesiae*. But...neither then nor later have I promised silence...in Rome people like to emphasize to a potential dissident that what he personally believes is of little interest to church authorities but that at least he should keep silent: *silentium obsequiosum*—obedient silence especially towards the Summus Pontifex.[1]

In the early fifties, as a theological student in Rome, Küng studied with the noted moral theologian Franz Hürth. Hürth's position, both in the classroom and later to Küng personally, was that "decency" required theologians to maintain a reverent silence when questioning the limits of the doctrine of infallibility. Küng noted that most theologians were wise and obediently kept silent. But not Küng: "So since I have the theological competence and more possibilities than others of raising the voice of conciliar renewal in the media, should I keep silent?"[2]

Anyone familiar with contemporary church life knows immediately that similar stress points between church authorities and theologians, pastoral ministers, and other church personnel are still very much present. Individuals have experienced a wide range of disciplinary actions from excommunication to loss of the title of "Catholic theologian." The modern stories have a similar ring to them: new initiatives in pastoral ministry arise based on personal experiences of ministers, new data from the human sciences is stressed by theologians addressing pressing theological issues, and new attempts to articulate alternate solutions to theological and pastoral problems are undertaken. As in the past, these attempts arouse suspicion or opposition from certain quarters; individuals are, to use a canonical term, "delated" to church authorities; cases are opened in the relevant Roman dicastery; investigators are appointed to examine writings; authors are required to respond to questions or meet for a personal interview; warnings are issued and eventually some action is taken. Many times the conflicts can be resolved on the local level with the aid of the local bishops' conference. At times, the result is a decisive intervention from higher authorities, usually after a long and sometimes complex procedure that is designed to guarantee a fair and just process.

The relationship between theologians and the magisterium has never seemed to recapture the harmonious experience of Vatican II when bishops and theologians worked side-by-side in mutual trust and respect. Rembert Weakland puts it well:

> My hope that there would be a renewal of theological investigation and a flowering of theological and philosophical inquiry in the Catholic Church, as there had been at Vatican II, never came about. On the contrary, tensions within the body of theologians and between them and the Holy See increased. After a period of time, it became evident that only certain theologians were favored, namely those who supported a particular, nar-

rower point of view like his [John Paul II's] own: the rest were shunted aside. It was noticeable that at synods of bishops, e.g., he invited to attend and speak only theologians and observers whose thinking never challenged his own. Dialogue was acceptable outside the Church, but not with it.[3]

Eventually several documents from Rome (*Instruction on the Ecclesial Vocation of the Theologian*, 1990) and the U.S. bishops (*Doctrinal Responsibilities: Approaches to Promoting Cooperation and Resolving Misunderstanding between Bishops and Theologians*, 1989) greatly helped clarify some of the procedural issues and provided workable solutions in many cases. Still, the ongoing situation of increasing numbers of theologians being investigated, censured, and punished, with methods that appear to lack some of the basic elements of what can be rightly called "due process," seem to echo the ecclesiastical dynamics at work in the stories of the four subjects of this work.

The revised procedures of the Congregation for the Doctrine of the Faith (*Regulations for the Examination of Doctrine*, 1997) have been seen as a modest reform of its rationale and procedures and they open to public scrutiny how the congregation actually determines the case of each theologian who has had an official case file opened. In many ways, it appears to be an exhaustively thorough and generally fair process, but the personal stories emanating from individuals who have experienced the process personally, seem to paint a different picture. Some have argued that when a particular individual or organization is the author, interpreter, and judge who oversees the writing, interpretation, and application of regulations pertinent to any judicial or administrative process against theologians or pastors, questions could be raised as to just how fair or unbiased such a procedure is.

In 2005, the Catholic Theological Society responded to the Vatican investigation of Roger Haight, SJ, by openly and seriously questioning whether the 1997 procedures of the CDF really do provide a theologian adequate opportunity to clear up "possible misunderstandings of his or her thought," as described in the 1990 document on the vocation of the Catholic theologian from the same congregation.

Any list of such individuals who might take this position over the past thirty years would include Hans Küng, Edward Schillebeeckx, Charles Curran, Leonardo Boff, Anthony Kosnik, Gustavo Gutiérrez, Karl Rahner, Ernesto Cardenal, John McNeill, André Guindon, Tissa Belasuriya, Matthew Fox, Bernard Haring, Anthony De Mello, Jacques Dupuis, William Callahan, Roger Haight, Paul Collins, Mary Agnes Mansour, and Ivone Gebara; Archbishops Marcel Lefebvre, Emmanuel Milingo, and Raymond Hunthausen; Bishops Jacques Gaillot and Thomas Gumbleton; and others whose names might not be as easily recognizable, even to the most ardent Vatican watchers. (Paul Collins recounts some of the personal stories of some of these individuals and their reactions to church discipline in *From Inquisition to Freedom: Seven Prominent Catholics and Their Struggle with the Vatican*, Continuum, 2001.) Each of those listed above responded to Rome's interventions and decisions in different ways. Some initially accepted a silencing (McNeill, Fox, and Boff), but eventually found that they were unable to remain silent and in violating the silencing order suffered the consequences of canonical expulsion from their religious orders or voluntary withdrawal.

Others, with the help of religious superiors and friends, were able to reverse a drastic punishment like excommunication (Belasuriya), while some simply accepted the final decision (Küng, Curran, Kosnick) though not always without strenuous attempts to prevent, reverse, or modify it. Two led their followers into formal schism. Some appeared to have suffered serious health problems related to the stress of the process (Guindon and Dupuis) and died before its conclusion. One underwent a lengthy investigation during a serious illness (Haring), but was still able to amount a convincing defense and had only to rewrite and clarify certain claims in his books that the congregation found objectionable and incompatible with authentic church teaching.

The individuals profiled in this work were all members of religious orders—two Jesuits, a Dominican, and a Trappist monk—all with vows of obedience that might have been a major factor in their ultimate willingness to accept and obey the final decision given to them directly by Rome or, more usually, indirectly through their religious superiors. More importantly, however, they lived in a time when public protests against perceived unjust treatment on the part of church authorities were unheard of. There were no organized letter-writing campaigns; mass-endorsed "open letters" of support in major publications; public-speaking appearances by punished theologians; and resolutions from professional organizations calling on church authorities to reconsider, amend, or rescind disciplinary actions taken against the theologians, pastoral workers, and even a few bishops. In a very few cases, these strategies seem to have had a positive effect on the outcome, but they are rare.

Another question that might be asked is whether anything positive could have been accomplished if the four theologians had resorted to strategies of public dissent employed by some theologians and their supporters in similar situations since Vatican II. Charles Curran, for one, believes that at least in the case of Congar:

> Perhaps reform would have been achieved more quickly if he would have resisted more actively or perhaps even left his ministry. Perhaps such spirituality is too passive and too easily accepts the imperfections and sinfulness of the institution and people in it. There are times when one cannot passively suffer, but must speak out boldly and resist the wrong that is being done.[4]

Curran acknowledges Congar's own belief that there is no meaning in suffering just for the sake of suffering and expresses admiration for Congar's own spirituality, which was strongly affected by what he suffered at the hands of ecclesiastical authorities.

Nevertheless, theologians today who find themselves at odds with the magisterium live in a vastly different ecclesial atmosphere and in a world culture dramatically transformed by the communications media. These changes provide new options to them that were not possible for theologians of a different historical period, although Merton and Murray, at least, surely had the wherewithal to mount public protests in their individual cases. Merton could have easily garnered support for himself by publicly protesting or even leaving the monastery and he did consider the possibility. Murray, on the other hand, was a very private person and, although he also had a large following in the academic community, seemed never to have considered a public protest. All four theologians in this study complained loudly and sometimes bitterly—but only privately to friends in conversations, letters, journals, or diaries. None ever "went public" with their personal side of the story, let alone organized support among their followers in the church.

However, the basic question remains: would such tactics have been successful or contributed to the overall goals of their theological and pastoral enterprises? Would Congar have been able to make any serious contribution to the shaping of important documents of the council had he decided to disobey the strictures put on his writing and publishing and left his order or the church? Would his writings have had the effect they have had if he had written "from outside," so to speak? Would a decision to leave his order or the church not have pleased Merton's strongest opponents and destroyed his credibility, as Merton suggested when musing on the possibility of freeing himself from monastic restrictions? The noted author and journalist, James Carroll, mused openly in a film based on his book *The Sword of Constantine*, asking himself: what would have happened had all the progressive priests of the Vatican II generation working for renewal and reform in the church stayed rather than leaving—would we see a much different church today?

Merton concluded that staying put in the monastery was the most effective way in which he could argue his case—from the center of the church. Would Murray have ever had the opportunity to see his lifelong work come to fruition in conciliar documents had he left the Jesuits to teach at a secular university and not been invited to the council? For Murray, his sober, quiet, and consistent style guaranteed that his position on religious freedom found a place in official teaching of the church. For Merton, his intellectual honesty, searing criticism of self and others, and loyalty to his vow of obedience, and his worldwide readership ensured that his arguments against nuclear war would become part of Catholic peacemaking. For Congar patience eventually was rewarded when his writings were reflected in many council documents. Only Teilhard seemed not to have lived to see some of his views infiltrate the thinking and interventions of some of the fathers and, perhaps, even documents of Vatican II. However, neither did he live long enough to see his writings once again the subject of an official "warning" from Rome. Ironically, this occurred just as the new winds of Vatican II began to be felt throughout the church, bringing with them a spirit of "openness to the world" and its materiality, which was such a central feature of Teilhard's creative thinking.

Today one might argue that defining "inside" and "outside" the church is perhaps not so easily done and, consequently, a theologian can be very effective even while not being institutionally "connected" in the academic or canonical sense. Surely, the cases of Küng and Curran show this. Being deprived of the title "Catholic theologian" might be a question of an inner-church language squabble for many who regard them still as among the best of Catholic theologians whose writings continue to impact the larger church community of which they are still very much a part both as priests and believers. Still, professional theologians and reform-minded Catholics would have rejoiced to have seen Curran hired as a professor by one of the other prestigious U.S. Catholic universities and deeply regretted the fact that none of them were courageous enough to do so.

What Teilhard, Congar, Murray, and Merton refused to do was to be marginalized. Perhaps this is a better way to approach the issue of "belonging" or "influencing" than talking about being inside or outside the church. Voices "from the margins" are by no means unimportant or ineffective, as proponents of liberation theology have amply demonstrated. Perhaps the same is true in the academic arena. These voices, theological or popular, are, at times, much freer to speak than others who are hampered by institutional ties.

But if the renewal of the institution itself, its teachings and pastoral practices that affect Catholics worldwide are among the theologian's main concerns, then the witness of their own position (e.g., priesthood, religious life, Catholic community, etc.) might be the most effective position within which to accomplish their objectives. Merton articulated this quite clearly as did Congar. Even Teilhard acknowledged that he felt he could not effectively contribute to the church what he wanted without his remaining attached to it and even through his vow of obedience.

For each remaining in the church and faithful to their vows of obedience was a real source of their strength and their ability to sustain continued assaults from many quarters on their theological and pastoral efforts. Teilhard, Congar, and Merton all wrestled with thoughts of abandoning their religious orders if not leaving the church entirely. All three of them decided in the end that such a move would do more harm than good. Murray, a very private person, seems not to have encountered any such temptation or, perhaps, never recorded or spoke of it. Undoubtedly strongly affected both emotionally and physically by his silencing, he opted to bide his time, as his Jesuit superiors had advised, until the time was ripe for the eventual official recognition and acceptance of his position.

Teilhard, Congar, and Merton were so completely "men of the church," in the best sense of that phrase, that they could not envision abandoning the family that had nourished both their faith and their theological talents. Perhaps they also had a good grasp of the history of the church and an insight into the way the Spirit works even, as Merton said, through the errors, foibles, and mistakes of superiors.

Although the word *scandal* is not much in use today, even in its technical theological sense, Teilhard, Congar, and Merton were each seriously concerned about the possibility of harming the faith of others by any precipitous actions of outright disobedience or leaving their orders or the church. Teilhard and Merton wrote specifically about this possibility and found it a convincing reason not to take any of those steps. Merton, more than any of the others, had a worldwide following and rumors had already circulated that he was planning or, actually, had left Gethsemani. The role that religious obedience played in his ultimate decision not to disobey or "bust out" as he termed it, however, did not prevent Merton from reflecting realistically on the authentic meaning and practice of the religious vow of obedience. He even worried that he might be cooperating in a false or unhealthy kind of obedience and distinguished between accepting an order under obedience from a superior and agreeing with the superior's reasoning for the order. In no sense was the obedience of any of the four "passive" or "uncritical."

The role of a religious vow of obedience might actually turn out to be the chief factor in the decisions of these men to accept various orders from religious superiors and Roman authorities. What might have occurred had they been diocesan priests (as are Küng and Curran) might have made a crucial difference in their decisions. For them, the vow was an integral part of their spirituality as was the personal hurt and pain they endured from the way they were viewed and treated by some ecclesiastical authorities and even some of their colleagues.

Since Vatican II and the renewal of the vowed religious life, all three vows have come under discussion and debate among theologians, religious formators, and others. New meanings have been suggested as to ways in which they can be interpreted and lived out purposefully and humanly in the present time. Some of these have been rejected by Roman congregations or papal addresses. At the same time, some of the newer insights into the theology and spirituality of the vow of obedience, the proper discernment of its prudent use and a deep realization of what it might cost an individual to fulfill it have found their way into official church documents.

Traditionally, the Jesuits are a special case since they take a fourth vow to be at the pope's disposal for church work—and recent popes have never been afraid to remind them publicly of that vow and call them back to an awareness of their special place in the church. Perhaps no other religious order in the church has placed so much emphasis on the vow of obedience as the Jesuits. Many theological and pastoral controversies since the council have involved members of the Society of Jesus.

Many of these conflicts between the Jesuits and the Vatican, including that of Jesuits holding political office in Nicaragua, occurred during the eighteen-year leadership of Pedro Arrupe. In 1981, the very popular father general suffered a stroke, and in 1983 was forced to resign. He was the first Jesuit father general to resign the leadership of the order instead of remaining in office until death.

The 33rd General Congregation was called to deal with the resignation and elect a new father general. Pope John Paul II appointed Father Paolo Dezza as the pontifical delegate to oversee the meeting and to assure that the Jesuits maintained their traditional loyalty to the pope. Many interpreted this as a sign of his displeasure with the Jesuits, a number of whom had been disciplined for their involvement in controversial theological or pastoral initiatives.

In a January 10, 2008, letter to then father general Peter-Hans Kolvenbach, Benedict XVI called on the Jesuits to reflect on obedience during their 35th General Congregation. Held in Rome from January 7 to March 6, the meeting had been called by the Jesuits to elect a new general and discuss issues of concern to the order. One result was to respond to the pope's letter. The Jesuit response was the decree "Obedience in the Life of the Society." It began with a direct reference to the pope: "Obedience is central to the mission and union of the Society of Jesus and a special bond of obedience links the Society to the Holy Father, 'the successor of St. Peter and vicar of Christ on earth,' as St. Ignatius was accustomed to call him."[5]

The statement faced up to the reality that freedom was, not the power to choose, so much as the power to order their choices to love:

> Commitment to the Word Incarnate cannot be separated from commitment to the concrete mediations of the Word that are at the center of our lives, the church and the society, which exists to serve the church. At times, however, our desire to commit ourselves to the Lord in personal trust is not matched by our desire to commit ourselves to the church or to the body of the society and its way or proceeding.[6]

The document goes on to describe what might have been comforting and strengthening to the Jesuits mentioned in this book and, especially, to Teilhard and Murray, when it speaks of "creativity" in carrying out their mission: "Ignatius...left much to their discretion...the society expects that Jesuits will exercise creativity in carrying out their mission as they see the circumstances require, that they will go beyond what has been asked in the true spirit of the *magis*."[7] In terms of theological "creativity," however, Benedict XVI has already expressed his opinion: "Every theologian now seems to want to be 'creative.' But his proper task is to deepen the common deposit of the faith as well as to help in understanding and proclaim it, not 'to create it.' "[8]

The *magis* is the seventh part of the Jesuit Constitutions on the foundational principle of obedience. The emphasis is on "discernment, freedom and creativity" in seeking God's will and in their apostolic ministry for the church.

Obedience is described as "creative" because "it calls on the individual's freedom and resourcefulness" and it is called "fidelity" because "it calls for a generous response to the directive of the superior whose duty it is to make decisions" according to the view in the Constitutions and for the good of those who are part of the institute."[9]

Quite by chance (or not) the Congregation for Institutes of Consecrated Life and Societies of the Apostolic Life published a lengthy document dated May 28, 2008, entitled "The Service of Authority and Obedience." This document also contains observations that the two Jesuits Teilhard and Murray would have easily recognized:

> For the consecrated person, it might also come to having "to learn obedience" through suffering or from some very specific and difficult situations: when, for example, one is asked to leave certain personal projects or ideas, to give up the pretext of managing one's life and mission by oneself; or all the times in which what is asked (or who asks it) does not seem to be very humanly convincing.[10]

Reminiscent of Teilhard's reflections on the role of obedience as mediated by ecclesiastical authority and the necessity of *sentire cum ecclesia*, the congregation reminds superiors that "our obedience is a believing with the church, a thinking and speaking with the church, serving through her."[11]

Both Teilhard and Murray personally embodied these principles long before they were articulated or recalled either by the Jesuits or the Vatican congregation. Merton's own understanding and practice of obedience reflected them as well. All four of them serve as models of an obedience that some might think no longer applicable in today's church. Certainly, theologians who chose to obey are not above criticism from their peers just as those who chose another path may be rightly challenged. All of the decisions around these issues are rather complex, very personal, and potentially life-changing. The impact on the life of any individual of a decision to obey or not and the repercussions on that decision in the life of the church are best left to history. From what we know of these four who chose to obey we can safely say that their discernment and decision proved personally to be very costly and their eventual vindication did little, perhaps, to assuage those painful memories and experiences. Indeed, that suffering was a crucial element in their spirituality. The lasting effects of their lives and writings on the modern church are clear evidence that they made the right choice for themselves.

If such theologians have a patron saint, it might just as well be the brilliant but sometimes reckless medieval theologian Abelard. While none of them suffered his horrendous punishment, they, like him, in their academic endeavors, attempted something new and did not keep their opinions to themselves. While they did not sign their own "death warrant," they did keep silent until "the time was ripe." A novel about Abelard's son, Astrolabe, captures it well:

Abelard dared to break new ground: He believed in a continuation of the revelation. He believed in a development. He believed that thought would always provide new openings. But for him thought meant not only rational argumentation, it meant awakening greater and greater human potential for interpreting the revelation in its various phases...for him thought meant listening more and more attentively to the *one* unfolding revelation....When I once spoke about it later with Abelard, my father, he said, It's better that you keep this opinion of yours to yourself; the time isn't ripe yet for this thought. And bear in mind that to fight for a new interpretation is to draw up and sign your own death warrant.[12]

Theologians today who are silenced continue, like their predecessors, to influence the thought and life of the church through their writings and witness to the church. Although they were condemned or silenced, they somehow managed to continue to contribute to the development of doctrine. Their ideas lived on, and, in some cases like Congar and Murray, became the cornerstones of Vatican II.

Silenced theologians do not deny the ministry of the teaching magisterium:

The notifications and instructions of the CDF can be and are often helpful theologically and pedagogically. The can and do contribute to continuing dialogue. They can and do demand and deserve the attention of other theologians. But when the congregation resorts to star-chamber tactics and political sanctions...the CDF may recapitulate the vicious politics of the early church.[13]

Terrence W. Tilley speaks of certain christological impasses such as the humanity and divinity of Christ and the salvific nature of non-Christian faiths that the CDF has attempted to resolve by certain tactics that have been found wanting. The major failed tactic is stopping a dialogue by silencing: "Stopping the dialogue by silencing theologians does not resolve impasse. You can kill theologians, but cannot silence them—sort of gagging their mouth and tying their hands behind them. Theologians keep writing and keep talking. The *habitus* of their vocation is too strong to be stopped by human authorities."[14]

Neither the congregations who repress writing and speaking nor theologians who refuse to rethink their positions contribute fruitfully to the resolution of impasses. The only valid alternative method, according to Tilley, that is adequate to get beyond the impasse whatever it is, is by staying "at the table no matter what until we can find a way together around the impasse."[15]

NOTES

Introduction

1. Congregation for the Doctrine of the Faith, "Instruction on the Ecclesial Vocation of the Theologian," *Origins* 20, no. 7 (1990): 117–126.

2. Francis A. Sullivan, "Magisterium," in *Dictionary of Fundamental Theology*, ed. René Lautourelle and Rino Fisichella (New York: Crossroad, 1994), 616.

Chapter One: Teilhard

1. Pierre Teilhard de Chardin, *Letters to Leontine Zanta*, trans. Bernard Wall (New York: Harper & Row, 1969), 102.

2. Ibid.

3. Ibid., 67.

4. Ibid.

5. Ibid., 29.

6. Ibid.

7. Robert Speaight, *The Life of Teilhard de Chardin* (New York: Harper & Row, 1967), 37.

8. Ibid., 138.

9. Teilhard, *Letters*, 139.

10. Speaight, *Life of Teilhard de Chardin*, 34.

11. Ibid., 140.

12. Ibid., 141.

13. Teilhard, *Letters*, 173–174.
14. Speaight, *Life of Teilhard de Chardin*, 93.
15. Ibid., 174.
16. Ibid., 30–31, 34.
17. Ibid., 30–31.
18. Ibid., 33.
19. Ibid., 32.
20. Teilhard, *Letters*, 323.
21. Ibid., 106.
22. Speaight, *Life of Teilhard de Chardin*, 40.
23. Peter Hebblethwaite, *Pope John XXIII: Shepherd of the Modern World* (NY: Image Books, 1987), 219.
24. Speaight, *Life of Teilhard de Chardin*, 21.
25. Ibid., 283.
26. Ibid.
27. Ibid., 284.
28. Ibid., 286.
29. Ibid., 260.
30. Hebblethwaite, *Pope John XXIII*, 422.
31. Giuseppe Alberigo, ed., *History of Vatican II*, vol. 4 (Maryknoll, NY: Orbis Books, 2003), 300.
32. Augustine Flannery, ed., *The Basic Sixteen Documents: Vatican Council II; Constitutions, Decrees, Declarations* (Northport, NY: Costello, 1996), 167.
33. Speaight, *Life of Teilhard de Chardin*, 323.
34. John R. Allen, Jr., "Pope Cites Teilhardian Vision of the Cosmos as a 'Living Host,'" *National Catholic Reporter*, July 28, 2009.

Chapter Two: Congar

1. Yves Congar, "Silenced for Saying Things Rome Didn't Like to Have Said," *National Catholic Reporter*, June 2, 2000.
2. Yves Congar, *Dialogue between Christians* (London: G. Chapman, 1996), 34.

3. Ibid., 44.

4. Ibid., 44, 45.

5. Ibid., 10.

6. Yves Congar, *Divided Christendom: A Catholic Study of the Problem of Reunion* (London: G. Bles, 1939), 36.

7. Ibid., 38.

8. Ibid.

9. Ibid., 39, 40.

10. Ibid., 41.

11. Hans Küng, *My Struggle for Freedom* (London: Continuum, 2002), 101.

12. Ibid., 104.

13. Ibid., 102.

14. Ibid., 112.

15. Congar, "Silenced for Saying Things," 3.

16. Yves Congar, "Easter Hope," *National Catholic Reporter*, April 21, 2002.

17. Thomas O'Meara, "Raid on the Dominicans: The Repression of 1954," *America* 170 (1994): 16.

Chapter Three: Murray

1. Donald E. Pelotte, *John Courtney Murray: Theologian in Conflict* (Mahwah, NJ: Paulist Press, 1975), 13.

2. Ibid., 25.

3. Ibid., 13.

4. Joseph A. Komonchak, "Catholic Principle and the American Experiment: The Silencing of John Courtney Murray," *Catholic Historian* 17 (1999): 31.

5. Pelotte, *John Courtney Murray*, 35.

6. Komonchak, "Catholic Principle," 31.

7. Ibid.

8. Pelotte, *John Courtney Murray*, 32.

9. Komonchak, "Catholic Principle," 32.

10. Pelotte, *John Courtney Murray*, 36.

11. Ibid.
12. Ibid., 64.
13. Ibid., 37.
14. Komonchak, "Catholic Principle," 42.
15. Pelotte, *John Courtney Murray*, 40.
16. Ibid. James Cardinal Gibbons (1834–1921) of Baltimore was the first cardinal in the United States and a national ecclesiastical and political figure of influence for many years. Known for his strong defense of labor unions and all things American, he was, however, always respectful but forthright in dealings with Rome. He actively defended the United States governmental model of the separation of church and state to Rome and believed the nation's constitution was the finest instrument of government ever created.
17. Ibid., 39.
18. Ibid.
19. Ibid., 41.
20. Ibid., 37.
21. Ibid., 38.
22. Ibid., 44.
23. Ibid.
24. Komonchak, "Catholic Principle," 34.
25. Ibid., 35.
26. Ibid.
27. Ibid., 35–36.
28. Ibid., 37.
29. Pelotte, *John Courtney Murray*, 53.
30. Komonchak, "Catholic Principle," 40.
31. Pelotte, *John Courtney Murray*, 52.
32. Ibid., 56.
33. Ibid.
34. Ibid., 59.
35. Ibid.
36. Ibid., 110.
37. Ibid., 85.
38. Gerald P. Fogerty, *The Vatican and the American Hierarchy from 1870 to 1965* (Stuttgart: Hiersemann, 1982), 395.

39. Xavier Rynn, *Vatican Council II* (Maryknoll, NY: Orbis Books, 1999), 460.

40. John W. O'Malley, "Vatican II: Did Anything Happen?" in *Vatican II: Did Anything Happen?* ed. David G. Schultenover (New York: Continuum, 2007), 58.

41. Joseph Ratzinger, "The Transmission of Divine Revelation," in *Commentary on the Documents of Vatican II*, ed. Herbert Vorgrimler (New York: Herder and Herder, 1969), 185.

42. Fogerty, *The Vatican*, 402.

43. James Carroll, *Practicing Catholics* (Boston: Houghton Mifflin, 2009), 85.

44. Robert McClory, "John Courtney Murray: Religious Freedom Triumphant," in *Faithful Dissenters: Stories of Men and Women Who Loved and Changed the Church* (Maryknoll, NY: Orbis Books, 2000), 23.

Chapter Four: Merton

1. Paul Wilkes, "Remembering Naomi Burton Remembering Tom: An Interview with Naomi Burton Stone," *The Merton Seasonal* 30 (2005): 13.

2. Victor A. Kramer, ed., *Turning toward the World: The Journals of Thomas Merton, 1960–1963*, vol. 4 (San Francisco: HarperSanFrancisco, 1996), 157.

3. Ibid., 182.

4. Ibid., 174.

5. Michael Mott, *The Seven Mountains of Thomas Merton* (Boston: Houghton Mifflin, 1984), 373.

6. Ibid., 360.

7. Ibid., 373.

8. Kramer, *Turning toward the World*, 213.

9. William H. Shannon, ed., *The Hidden Ground of Love* (New York: Farrar, Straus, Giroux, 1985), 351.

10. Mott, *Seven Mountains of Thomas Merton*, 374.

11. Ibid., 375.

12. Patrick Hart, ed., *The School of Charity* (New York: Farrar, Straus, Giroux, 1990), 142.

13. Mott, *Seven Mountains of Thomas Merton*, 377.

14. Hart, *School of Charity*, 216.

15. Shannon, *Hidden Ground of Love*, 266.

16. Hart, *School of Charity*, 142.

17. Ibid., 143.

18. Shannon, *Hidden Ground of Love*, 398.

19. Ibid., 573.

20. Mott, *Seven Mountains of Thomas Merton*, 385.

21. Ibid., 379–380.

22. Shannon, *Hidden Ground of Love*, 267.

23. Patricia A. Burton, "The Book that Never Was: 'Peace in the Post-Christian Era'" (report, John M. Kelly Library, University of Saint Michael's College, Toronto, Canada, 1980), 11.

24. Ibid.

25. Shannon, *Hidden Ground of Love*, 74.

26. Ibid., 269.

27. Ibid., 270.

28. Kramer, *Turning toward the World*, 244–245.

29. Hart, *School of Charity*, 166.

30. Burton, "The Book That Never Was," 12.

31. Shannon, *Hidden Ground of Love*, 447.

32. Ibid., 609.

33. Ibid, 497.

34. Thomas Merton, *A Vow of Conversation* (New York: Farrar, Straus, Giroux, 1988), 64.

35. Shannon, *Hidden Ground of Love*, 267.

36. Burton, "The Book That Never Was," 7.

37. William H. Shannon, ed., *Witness to Freedom* (New York: Farrar, Straus, Giroux, 1994), 143.

38. Kramer, *Turning toward the World*, 318.

39. Merton, *Vow of Conversation*, 28.

40. Shannon, *Hidden Ground of Love*, 267.

41. Ibid., 267–268.

42. Thomas Merton, *Thomas Merton in Alaska* (New York: New Directions, 1988), 134, 136, 137.
43. Rembert G. Weakland, *A Pilgrim in a Pilgrim Church* (Grand Rapids, MI: Eerdmans, 2009), 166.
44. James Harford, *Merton and Friends* (New York: Continuum, 2006), 290.

Epilogue

1. Hans Küng, *Disputed Truth: Memoirs II* (New York: Continuum, 2007), 410.
2. Ibid., 431.
3. Rembert G. Weakland, *A Pilgrim in a Pilgrim Church* (Grand Rapids, MI: Eerdmans, 2009), 404.
4. Charles Curran, *Loyal Dissent Memoirs of a Catholic Theologian* (Washington, DC: Georgetown University Press, 2006), 245.
5. Jesuit General Congregation, "Jesuit Decree: Obedience in the Life of the Society," *Origins* 38, no. 7 (2008): 104.
6. Ibid., 107.
7. Ibid.
8. Joseph Ratzinger, *The Ratzinger Report* (San Francisco: Ignatius Press, 1985), 71.
9. Ibid., 107.
10. Congregation for Institutes of Consecrated Life and Societies of Apostolic Life, "The Service of Authority and Obedience," *Origins* 38, no. 5 (2008): 71.
11. Ibid., 73.
12. Luise Rinser, *Abelard's Love*, (Lincoln, NE: University of Nebraska Press, 1998), 90–91.
13. Terrence W. Tilley, "Three Impasses in Christology," *Origins* 39, no. 7 (2009): 101.
14. Ibid.
15. Ibid.

SELECTED BIBLIOGRAPHY

Chapter One: Chardin

DeLubac, Henri. *Teilhard de Chardin: The Man and His Meaning.* Translated by René Hague. New York: New American Library, 1965.

Grenet, Paul Bernard. *Teilhard de Chardin: The Man and His Theories.* Translated by R. A. Rudorff. New York: P. S. Eriksson, 1966.

Lukas, Mary and Ellen Lukas. *Teilhard: The Man, the Priest, the Scientist.* New York: Doubleday, 1977.

Speaight, Robert. *The Life of Teilhard de Chardin.* New York: Harper & Row, 1967.

Teilhard de Chardin, Pierre. *Letters to Leontine Zanta.* Translated by Bernard Wall. New York: Harper & Row, 1967.

Chapter Two: Congar

Congar, Yves. *Dialogue between Christians.* Translated by Philip Loretz. London: G. Chapman, 1996.

————. *Lay People in the Church.* Translated by Donald Attwater. London: G. Chapman, 1965.

————. *Power and Poverty in the Church.* Translated by Jennifer Nicholson. London: G. Chapman, 1964.

————. *Report from Rome: On the First Session of the Vatican Council.* Translated by A. Mason. London: G. Chapman, 1963.

————. *Report from Rome II: The Second Session of the Vatican Council.* Translated by L. Sheppard. London: G. Chapman, 1964.

Chapter Three: Murray

Fogerty, Gerald P. *The Vatican and the American Hierarchy from 1870 to 1965.* Stuttgart: Hiersemann, 1982.

Hughes, Emmet John. "A Man for Our Season." *The Priest* 25 (1969).

Komonchak, Joseph A. "Catholic Principle and the American Experiment: The Silencing of John Courtney Murray." *Catholic Historian* 17 (1999).

McClory, Robert. *Faithful Dissenters: Stories of Men and Women Who Loved and Changed the Church.* Maryknoll, NY: Orbis Books, 2000.

Pelotte, Donald E. *John Courtney Murray: Theologian in Conflict.* Mahwah, NJ: Paulist Press, 1975.

Chapter Four: Merton

Forest, Jim. *Living with Wisdom: A Life of Thomas Merton.* Maryknoll, NY: Orbis Books, 1991.

Furlong, Monica. *Merton: A Biography.* New York: Harper & Row, 1980.

Griffin, John Howard. *The Hermitage Journals.* Edited by Conger Beasley, Jr. Kansas City, KS: Andrews and McMeel, 1981.

Merton, Thomas. *The Seven Storey Mountain.* New York: Harcourt, Brace, 1948.

Mott, Michael. *The Seven Mountains of Thomas Merton.* Boston: Houghton Mifflin, 1984.

The Battle for Rights in
the United States Catholic Church
Kevin E. McKenna

Recounts the work of several controversialists in
nineteenth-century United States in defending the rights of
priests and pushing toward reform for all Catholics in
church governance, including more voice in Episcopal
appointments and greater accountability to the laity in
parish and diocesan finances.

978-0-8091-4493-8 Paperback
www.paulistpress.com

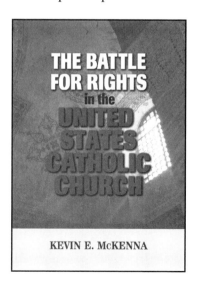

The Great Catholic Reformers
From Gregory the Great to Dorothy Day
C. Colt Anderson

Lessons on church reform for today from ten of the most
significant reformers in church history.

978-0-8091-0579-3 Hardcover
www.paulistpress.com

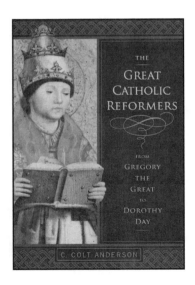

Teilhard's Mass
Approaches to "The Mass on the World"
Thomas M. King, SJ

A study of Teilhard's "Mass on the World" that enables
all Christians to assume their priesthood and transform
both their life and their death into an all-embracing Mass
on the Altar of the World.

0-8091-4328-3 Paperback
www.paulistpress.com

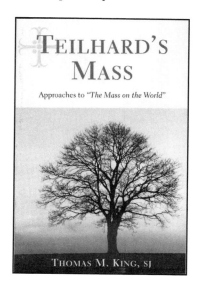

Teilhard de Chardin -
The Divine Milieu Explained
A Spirituality for the 21st Century
Louis M. Savary

A series of groundbreaking spiritual methods that integrate science and faith according to the evolutionary spirituality of Teilhard de Chardin's *The Divine Milieu*.

978-0-8091-4484-6 Paperback
www.paulistpress.com

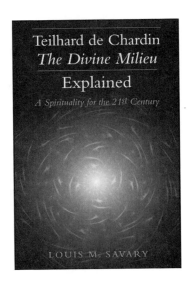

The New Spiritual Exercises
In the Spirit of Pierre Teilhard de Chardin
Louis M. Savary

This book presents a spiritual renewal system for contemporary believers based on Ignatius' Spiritual Exercises and inspired by the modern insights of Jesuit priest-scientist Pierre Teilhard de Chardin.

978-0-8091-4695-6 Paperback
www.paulistpress.com

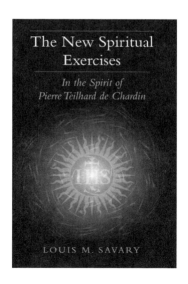

The Legacy of Pierre Teilhard de Chardin
Edited by James Salmon, SJ, and John Farina

The book is a testimony to the spiritual, theological, and scientific legacy of Pierre Teilhard de Chardin.

978-0-8091-4682-6 Paperback
www.paulistpress.com

Teilhard de Chardin and Eastern Mysticism
Ursula King; Preface by Joseph Needham

An in-depth examination of Teilhard de Chardin's knowledge of the Middle and Far East, especially China, his comments on eastern religions, and his comparative reflections on mysticism and spirituality.

978-0-8091-4704-5 Paperback
www.paulistpress.com

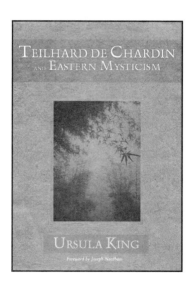

Thomas Merton:
Spiritual Master
edited by Lawrence S. Cunningham

A one-volume anthology of the spiritual writings of the greatest spiritual master the American Catholic church has produced in this century. The selections, which are substantial in length, provide a generous sampling of Merton's vast output.

0-8091-3314-8 Paperback
www.paulistpress.com

THOMAS MERTON:
SPIRITUAL MASTER

THE ESSENTIAL WRITINGS
EDITED, WITH AN INTRODUCTION
BY LAWRENCE S. CUNNINGHAM
FOREWORD BY PATRICK HART, O.C.S.O.
PREFACE BY ANNE E. CARR

Walking with Thomas Merton
Discovering His Poetry, Essays, and Journals
Robert Waldron; foreword by Patrick Hart, OCSO

An appreciation, in journal form, of Thomas Merton as
spiritual writer, monk, and poet.

0-8091-4058-6 Paperback
www.paulistpress.com

Thomas Merton - Master of Attention
An Exploration of Prayer
Robert Waldron

Fully explores the inner life of perhaps the best-known writer on prayer of the twentieth century.

978-0-8091-4521-8 Paperback
www.paulistpress.com

Becoming Who You Are
Insights on the True Self from Thomas Merton and Other Saints
James Martin, SJ

By meditating on personal examples from the author's life, as well as reflecting on the inspirational life and writings of Thomas Merton, stories from the Gospels, and the lives of other holy men and women (among them, Henri Nouwen, Therese of Lisieux and Pope John XXIII), the reader will see how becoming who you are, and becoming the person that God created, is a simple path to happiness, peace of mind and even sanctity.

1-58768-036-X Paperback
www.paulistpress.com

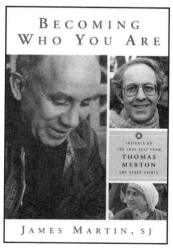

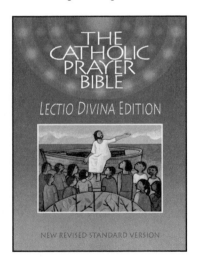

The Catholic Prayer Bible (NRSV):
Lectio Divina Edition
Paulist Press

An ideal Bible for anyone who desires to reflect on the
individual stories and chapters of just one, or even all, of
the biblical books, while being led to prayer though
meditation on that biblical passage.

978-0-8091-0587-8 Hardcover
978-0-8091-4663-5 Paperback
www.paulistpress.com